# ABANDONED OKLAHOMA

## CONSOLIDATED DIST. NO. 5

JAKE DURHAM

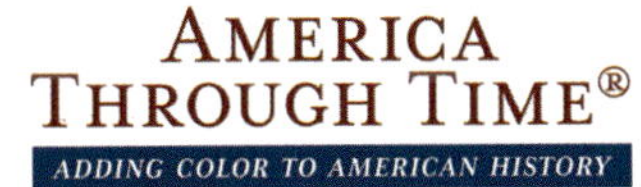

*For my children,*
*who fought and survived the boredom*
*associated with countless hours of my relentless photography.*
*Yet, each found their way to be part of the journey*
*and participate in the excitement of exploration.*

America Through Time is an imprint of Fonthill Media LLC
www.through-time.com
office@through-time.com

Published by Arcadia Publishing by arrangement with Fonthill Media LLC
For all general information, please contact Arcadia Publishing:
Telephone: 843-853-2070
Fax: 843-853-0044
E-mail: sales@arcadiapublishing.com
For customer service and orders:
Toll-Free 1-888-313-2665

www.arcadiapublishing.com

First published 2021



ISBN 978-1-63499-363-0



Typeset in Trade Gothic
Printed and bound in England

# CONTENTS

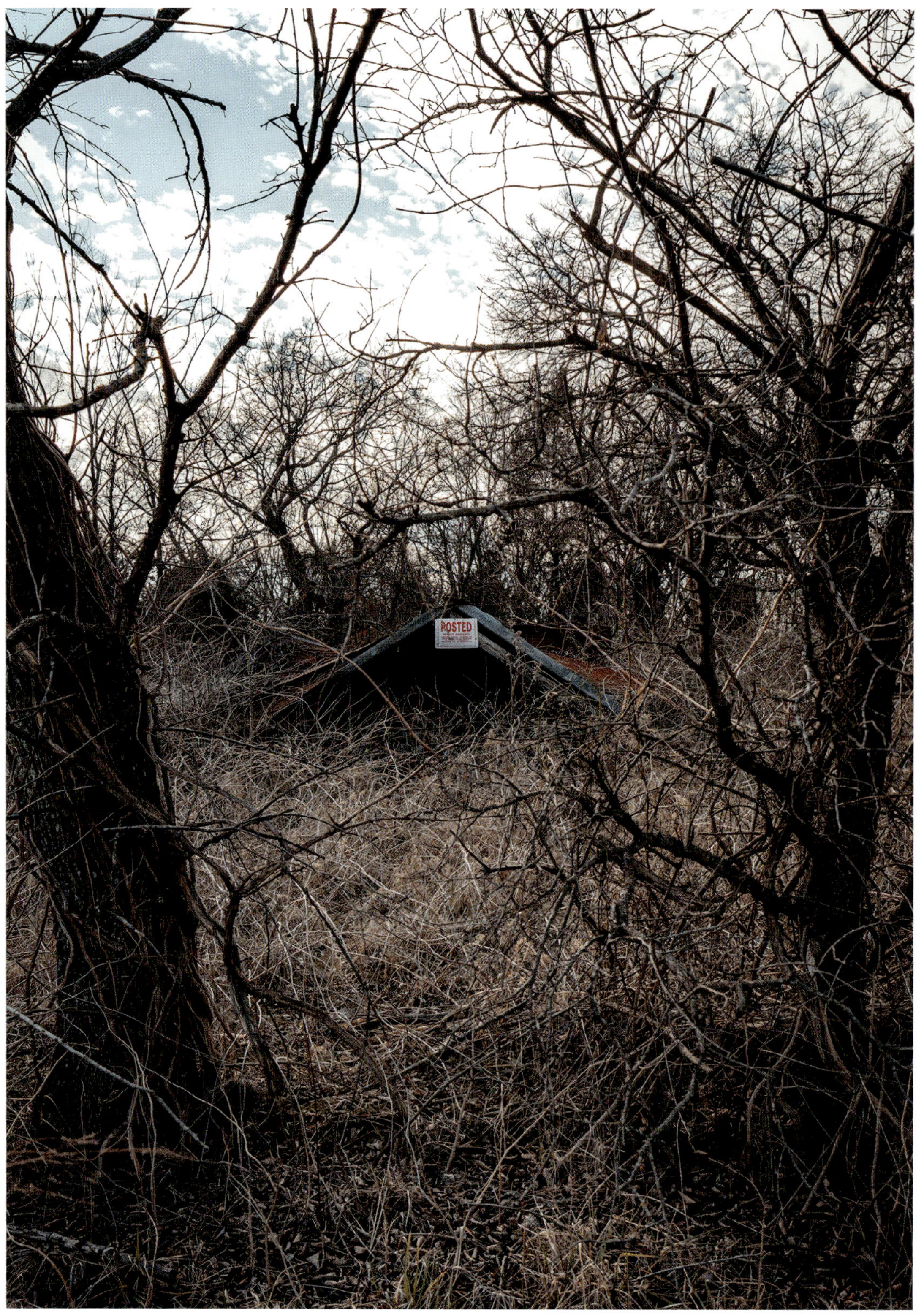


A look into the past.

# PREFACE

I have fond memories of my childhood. I remember the days of walking to school: no buses, no rides from my parents—rain, shine, and floods of biblical proportions could not thwart my attendance. I was raised in an era where I could tell the tale to my children about the days of walking to school at least a mile, if not more, in the snow.

I was unaware of the political driving forces behind drawing district lines, closing schools, and, in some cases, segregating students. Residential zoning often determined the quality of education and funding for a given institution. But as a kid, we never thought of such things.

School was a place to hang out with friends, get into trouble, and have your first crush. We had in-class birthday, Christmas, and Valentine's Day parties. We ditched class, played pranks—it was a place to be a kid. While you may have been aware of some inequalities that plagued fellow classmates, they were often quickly handled by the school or others in the community. That was the outward appearance, at least.

I remember friends not being well dressed, not having supplies, not bringing lunch, or having money to purchase lunch on a particular day. But someone always stepped in. Today, however, the news seems to be filled with stories of students sent home because of their clothes. Being denied lunch because of a lack of financial means. More recently, I have heard of stories of students being suspended because of what they wore or what transpired in the background during a Zoom class.

The value of education in America is changing, but the battle for quality schools and educating the masses has always been a struggle. It seems that society holds less value on education than when I was younger. However, one needs not look far to find articles and books that describe many modern school horrors in America.

Schools are consolidating or closing at an alarming rate. While these practices are not new, the trends appear to be.

Many politicians dislike public education. This is not a secret, and some will openly admit to it. Several years ago, I attended an event at the Oklahoma state capitol for educators. Higher education was there to support an upcoming vote for more funding amid a barrage of budget cuts. The group spoke to one of the representatives after he voted down the measure—a measure which he assured those in the district that he, and the State Legislature, would vote in favor of. When pressed for answers, the response was blunt: "Politicians hate public education." They are afraid of it, and they are fearful of those who are educated.

States have an array of means to defund education. Rezoning is one of the more popular methods. Revoking funds and rebudgeting are others. In Boley, Oklahoma, a county correctional facility was placed immediately adjacent to the town contributing to the dissolution of the local economy. Coincidently, Boley was a pioneer all-Black town in the state.

Harjo Consolidated Dist. No. 5 became one more statistic in the decay of the American education system. Institutions like Harjo once were, and often still are, staples in rural communities and among those that served African Americans, Native Americans, the disenfranchised, and the poor. As these institutions closed down, many students found themselves forced to travel significant distances to continue their education or forgo it altogether. Harjo was no different, and it provided services to several cities within the locale.

Conceived during Oklahoma's oil boom, Harjo was hailed as one of the finest schools of its kind by the late 1920s. However, the institution faltered almost as quickly as it rose. Many remaining alumni have fond memories of their tenure at Harjo, but as time passes, their numbers dwindle, and the institution fades. Not without effort, attempts to repurpose the facility have been implemented, though Harjo never returned to its full glory. This is a pictorial documentary of what remains of Harjo, and it is one of many tales of America's struggle with inequality and the education system.

# 1

# DON'T BLINK

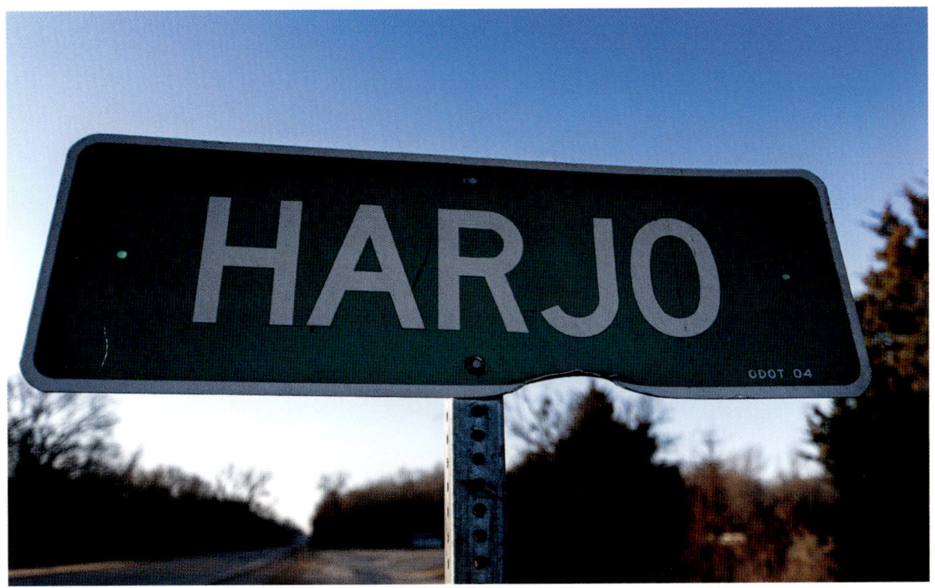


Don't blink, or you'll miss it—quite literally. You would never know, passing through rural Pottawatomie county, that the little town of Harjo exists. That is unless you are from this part of Oklahoma. Harjo is just one more dot on a map that most Oklahoma residents are unaware of. However, these once-bustling communities are beginning to fade as the years press on. All but the last of their fiercely devoted residents remain. Yet towns like Harjo make up portions of America that many will never see.

Very little information exists about the town; however, a Google search turns up small bits and pieces. Harjo is commonly used as a surname. It is also derived from the Muscogee Creek word *Hadchado* meaning "crazy" or "so brave as seems to be crazy." The town of Harjo is a small community that lies south of Shawnee, Oklahoma, and is one of the numerous communities that form Pottawatomie county. Harjo was settled in the early 1900s; however, it was never incorporated. In the 1920s, the *Tecumseh Oil Record* identified Harjo as an oil-boom town. One never would have guessed passing by it.

In 1929, the *Tecumseh Oil Record* reported that as many as 3,000 residents lived in Harjo. However, like so many other small towns in Oklahoma, Harjo began to die as the oil dried up. Newspaper clippings describe a notable community that boasted a post office, a cement plant, and even inspired the state to pave new highways, which joined it to other towns such as Maud, St. Louis, Asher, Tecumseh, and Earlsboro. At one time, rail services passed through the area.[1]

I drove by the town daily. In fact, I seldom paid attention to the structures that often flitted in the corner of my eye. However, that changed one day when I decided to take a detour and drive down one of the local streets. The town was smaller than I imagined and a far cry from the once 3,000 residents. A handful of homes are just off the main highway, one of which is in disarray. Next to it, another abandoned structure.

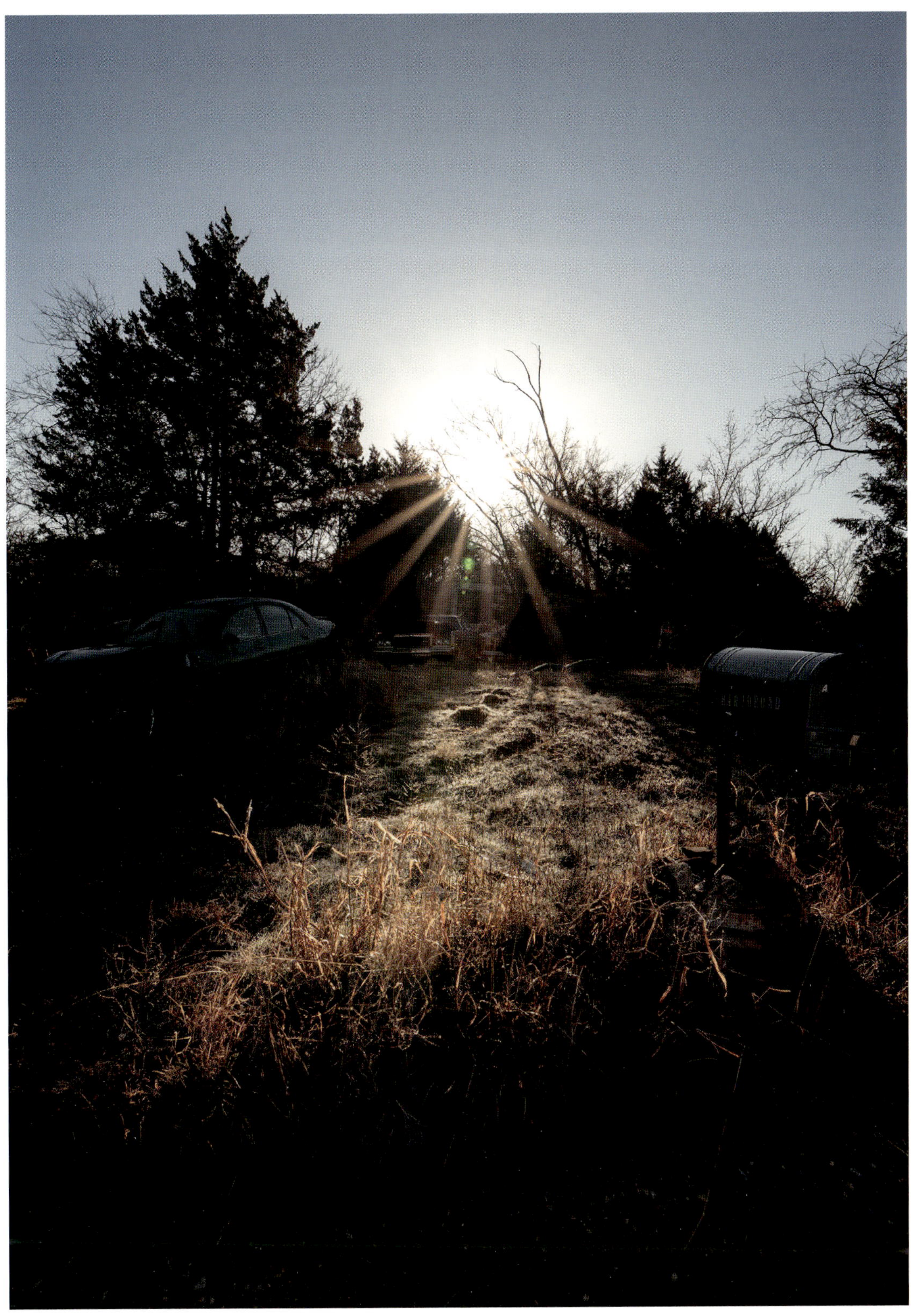

A place to call home.

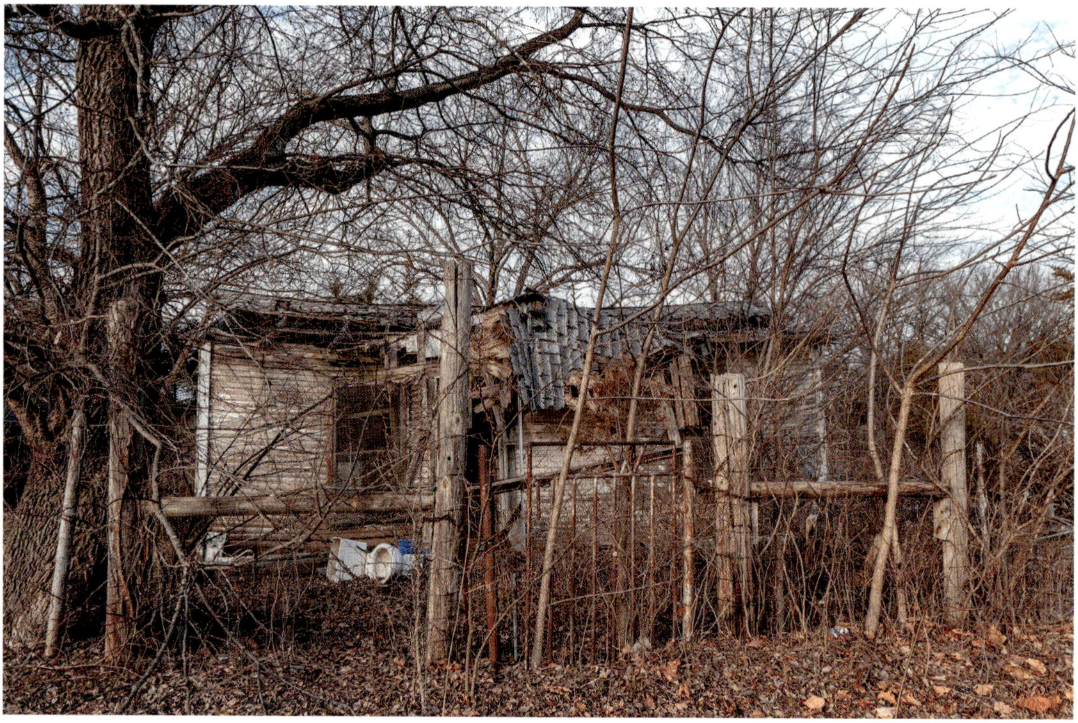

For mother.

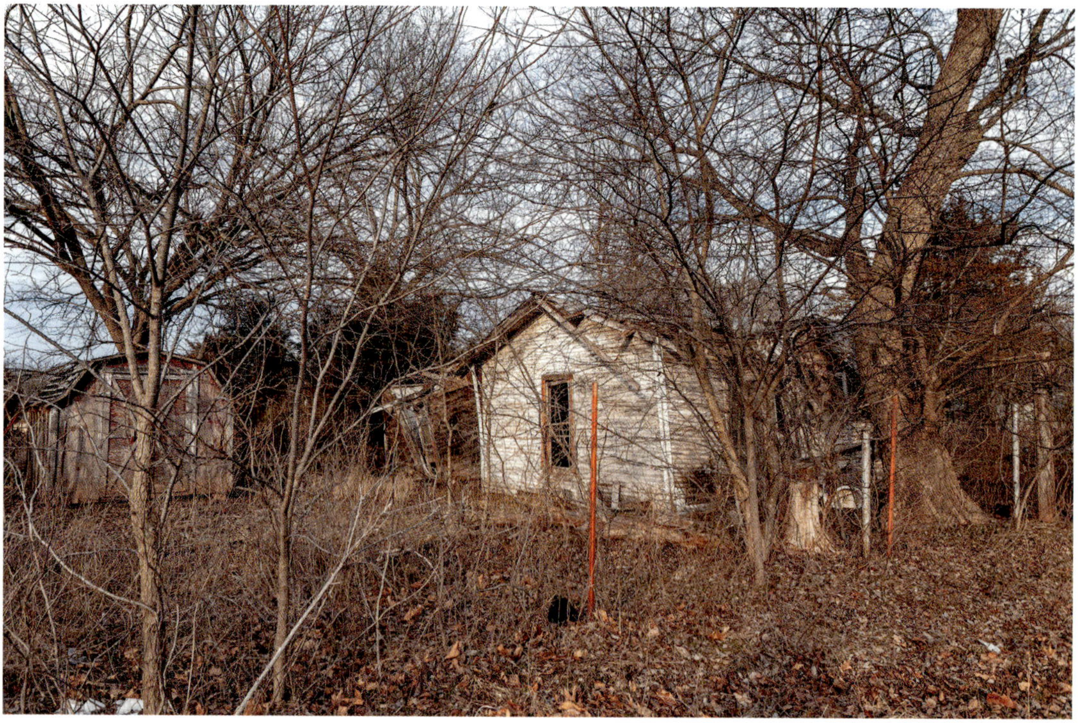

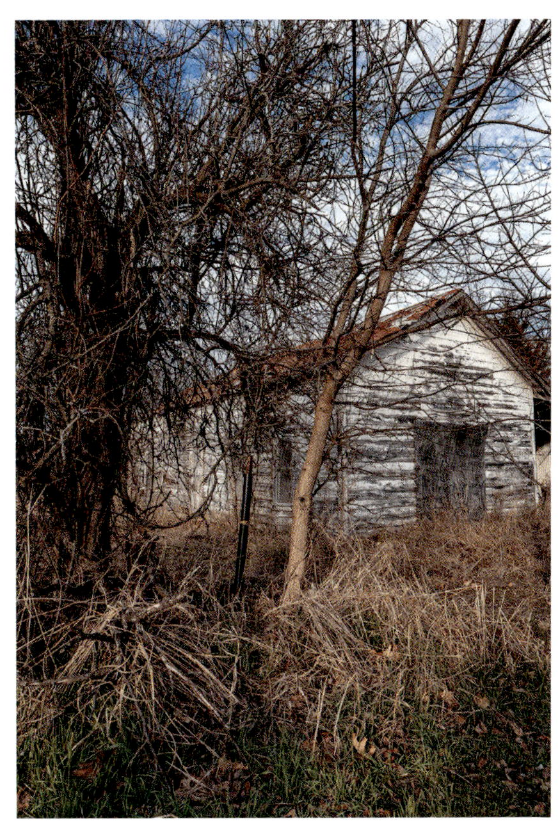

A once prominent but now abandoned church.

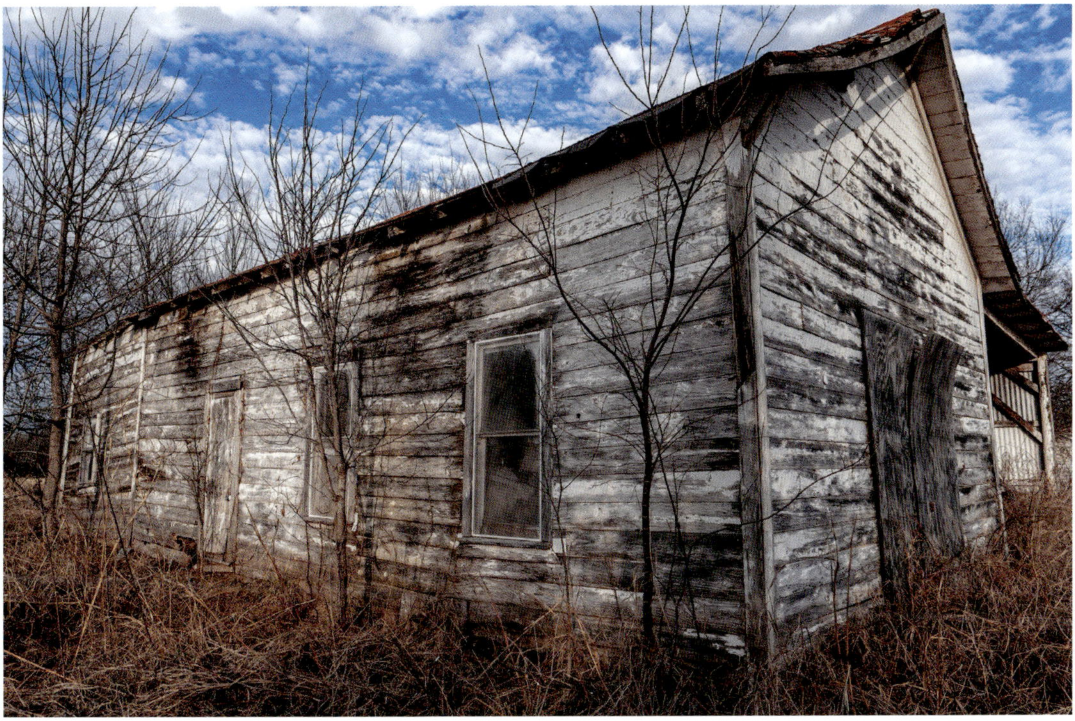

I decided to stop and take photos, which drew the attention of a local resident who was more than curious regarding my presence. Many rural communities form tight-knit bonds. Everyone really does know everyone else. People still wave to one another, and you can leave your door unlocked or your belongings about without fear or hesitation. The neighbor was kind enough to tell me a little about the property I was enamored with and explained that the larger building was once a church, while the house next door was built for the pastor's mother. Neither of them is close to what they once were, and local residents would like to see both torn down.

Satisfied with my new discovery and artistic images, I departed. But something about the town continued to stoke my curiosity. For the next few days, I grew more conscious about other structures on the highway as I traveled to and from. I noted a few different homes scattered across the landscape aside from the cluster located on the north end of town. One spot in particular, on top of a hill, was an old stone building that resembled a CCC (Civilian Conservation Corps) project.

I conducted this ritual for a few weeks before finally deciding to look at a satellite image of the town. Not surprisingly, I saw nothing more than what I could see from the road. The town was barren. At first glance, I would have guessed that no more than seven to ten houses remained. I quickly located the stone building; and something else. It was massive. To me, it was something that should not belong there.

# 2

# HARJO CONSOLIDATED DIST. NO. 5

What was it? I could not wait to find out. Why was such a massive building located in the middle of a town that is almost non-existent? It was a Saturday morning, and I assumed that now was a good time to go exploring. I took a side road off the highway and shot straight for the stone building. As I crested the top of the hill, the larger structure that appeared on satellite came into view. A school! An abandoned school in the middle of nowhere.

I love abandoned schools. They are more fascinating to me than any other abandoned structure. I eagerly pulled up to the school and started to get out when I noticed I had drawn the attention of a few residents. I was being watched closely. So, I circled the facility a few times to get a better look. Eventually, I summoned the courage to walk the grounds and peer through the windows.

"Consolidated Dist. No. 5," it says, just above the main entrance. There are homes on all sides of the school, and they are close enough that any one of the neighbors could be next to me before I had the opportunity to blink. While the school did not appear to be heavily vandalized, it was unkept other than the main grounds. The building had been in disarray for some time. It is a single-level construction and in a z-shaped pattern. Several windows were broken or missing, but that is typical of many abandoned locations.

I peered into as many of the openings as possible and wondered how long it would take before a neighbor approached me to question why I was there. I snapped a few quick photos of the building from the outside, gave a light tug on a few doors, and went back home disappointed but excited. I was determined to learn more about the facility and its history.

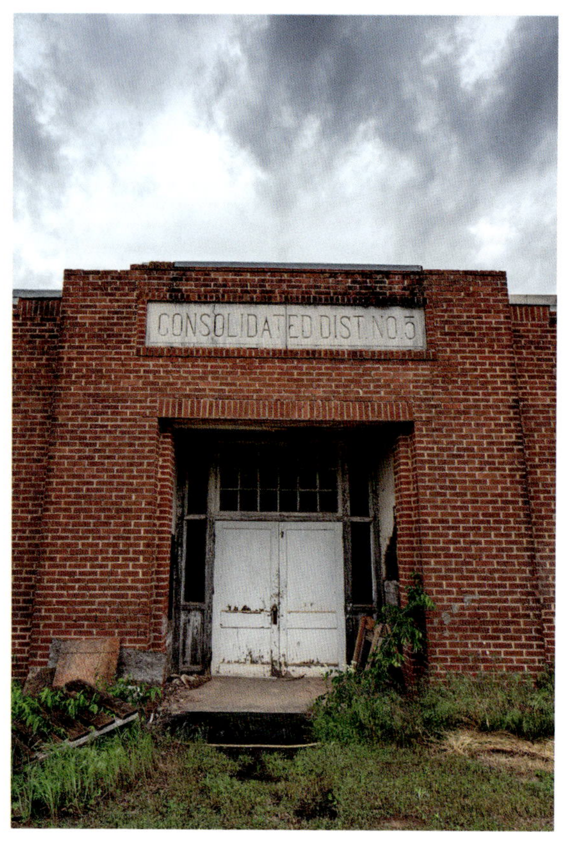


*Left:* Harjo Consolidated Dist. No. 5.

*Below:* Harjo's main entrance.

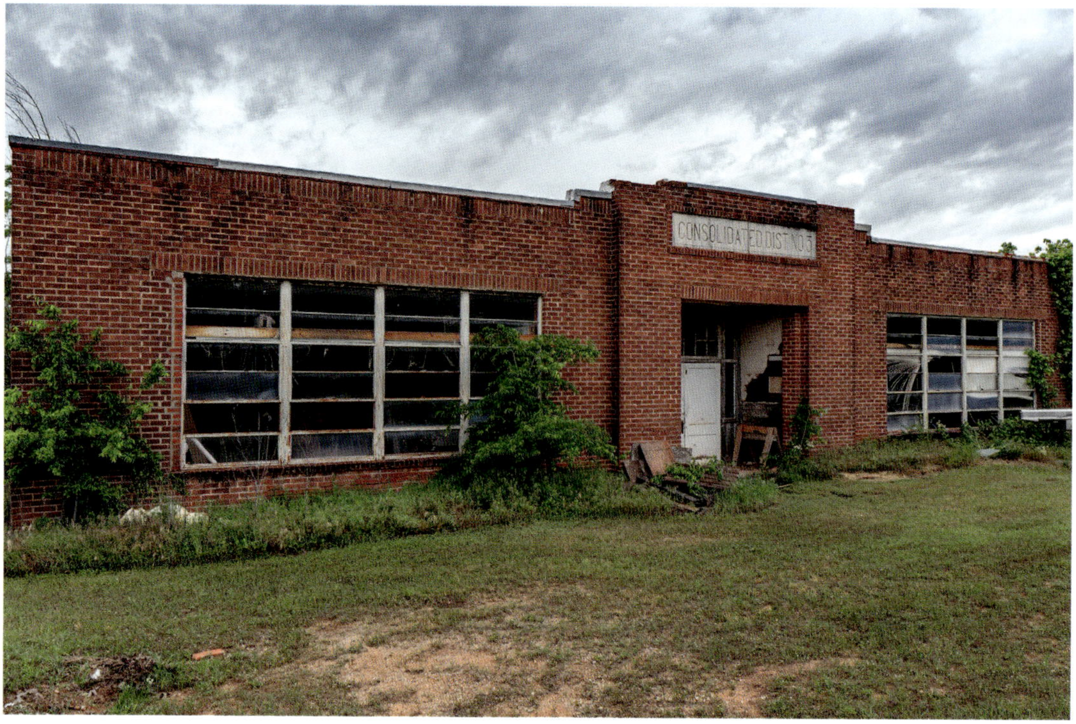

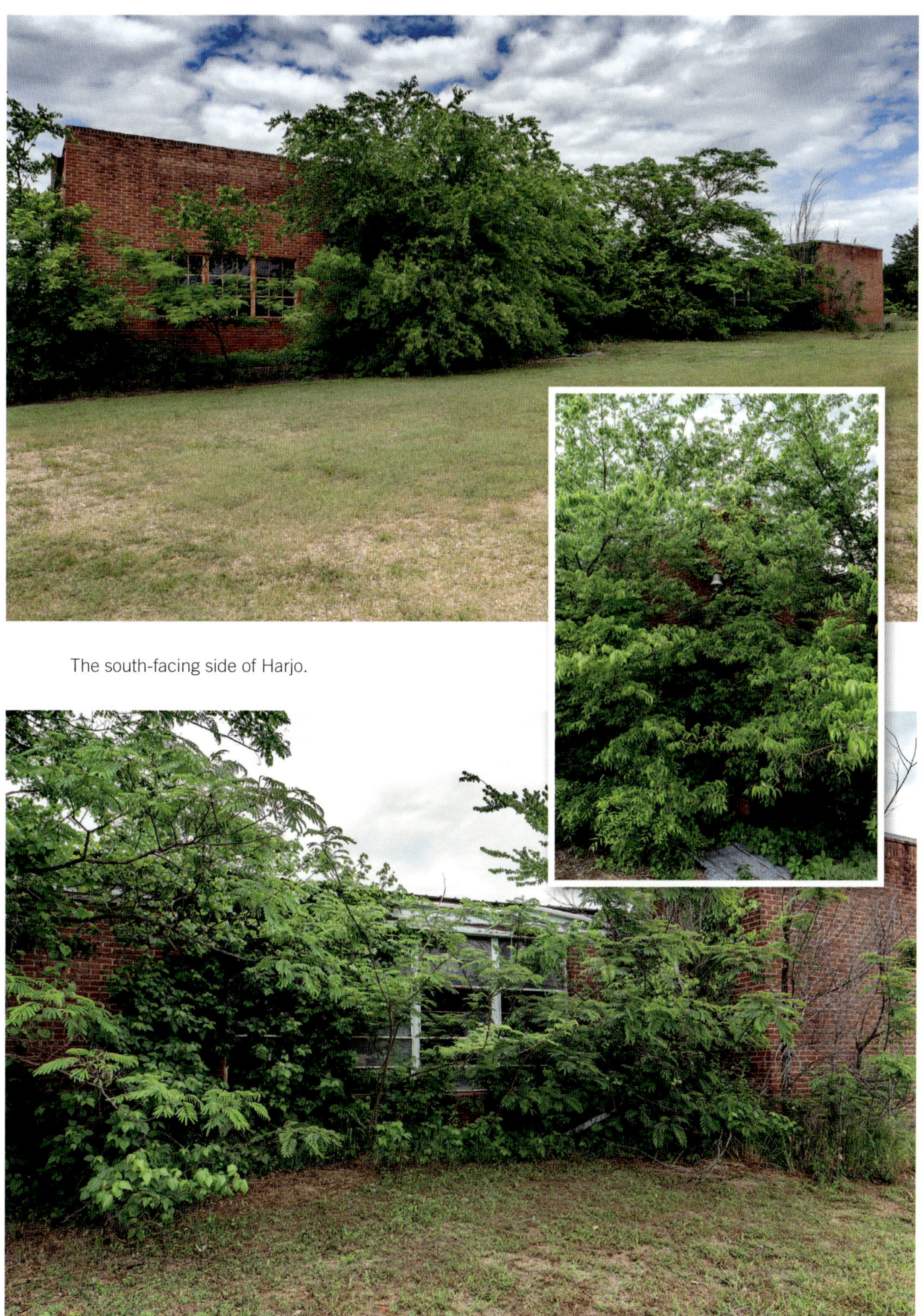

The south-facing side of Harjo.

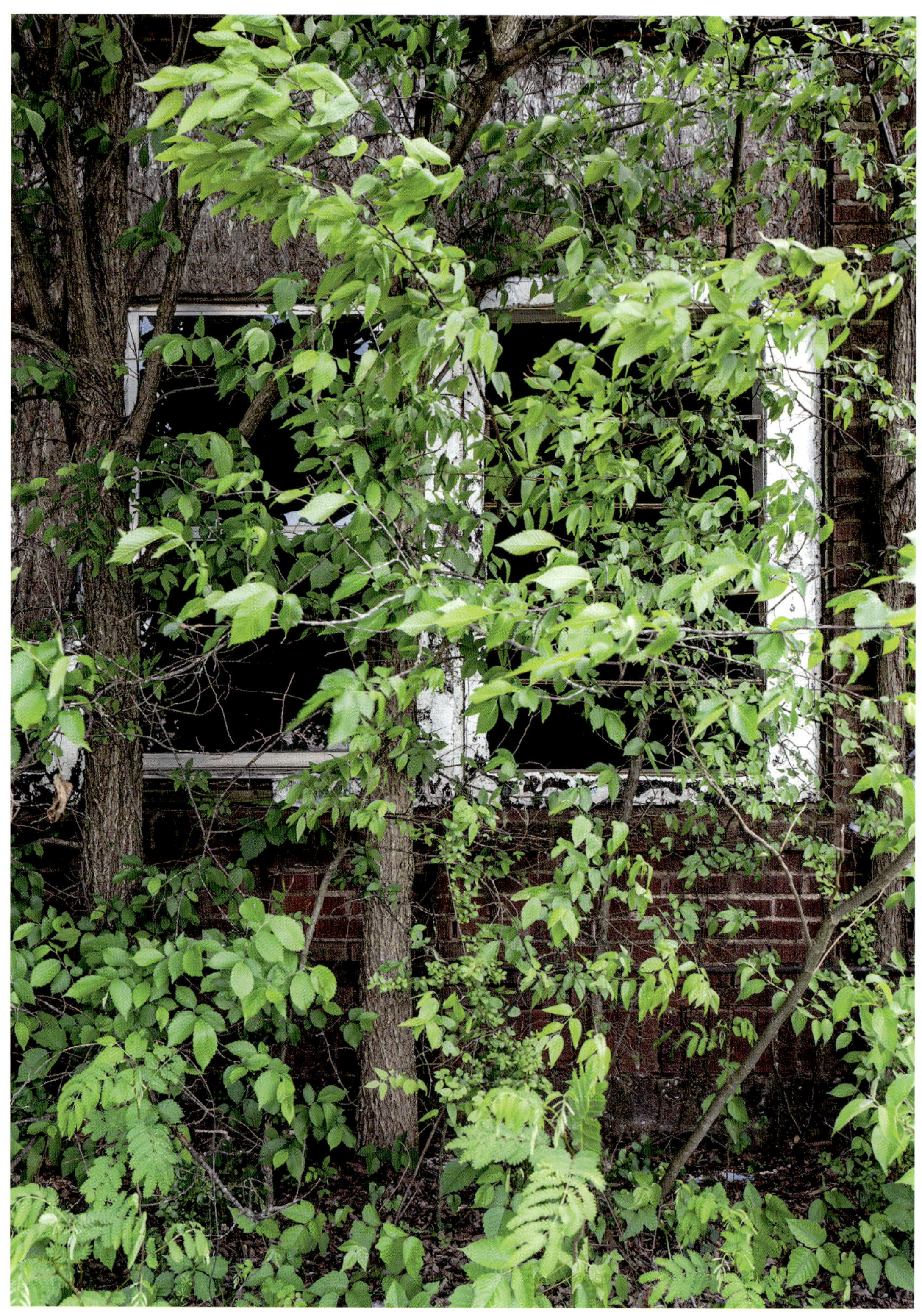

A north-facing window overgrown with vegetation.

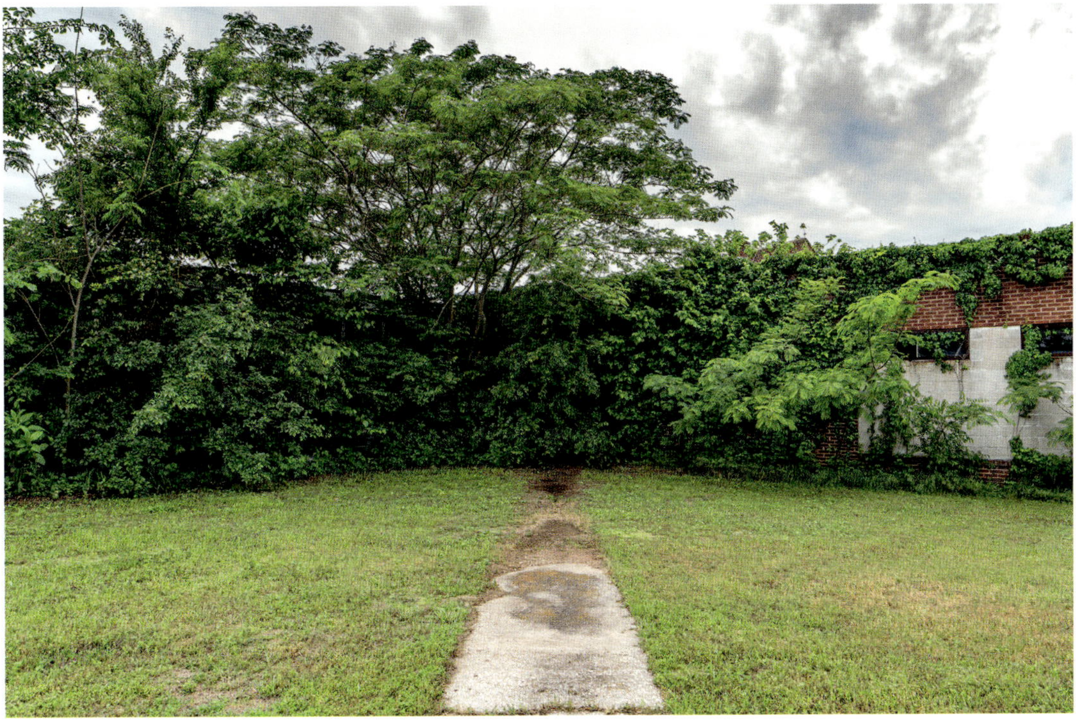

North-facing rooms and Harjo's east entrance.

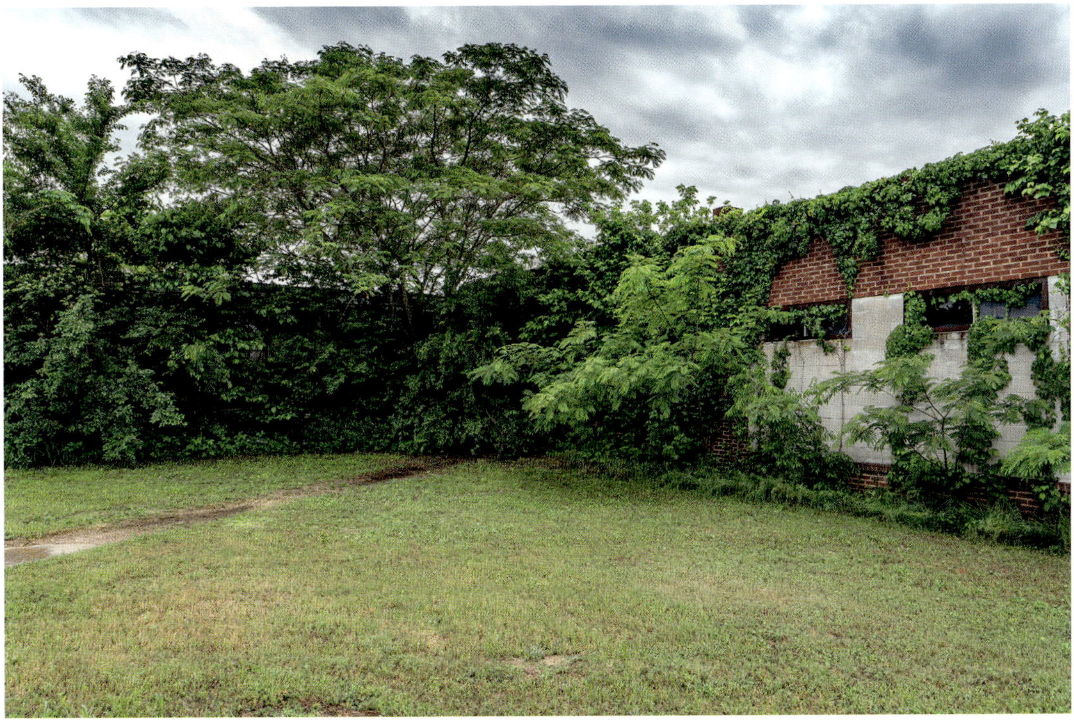

Through some sleuthing, I was able to locate the owner, who was more than gracious enough to provide me a brief history about the school, along with permission to come back and document the facility. However, even after our initial encounter, I was left with more questions than answers. Harjo was abandoned in the late 1960s. It seemed that the institution disappeared almost as mysteriously as it materialized. Here one day and gone the next.

## "Harjo Has Excellent School"

Buried in a column on page five of the February 14, 1929 edition of the *Tecumseh Oil Record*, it reads, "Harjo Has Excellent School." Aside from newspaper clippings, little is known about the school or town. However, one article describes the school in its splendor, which also indicated that Harjo was far superior compared to surrounding institutions. It was hailed as a modern facility with seven rooms that served over 300 students.[1]

In the same editorial, *The Record* noted that Harjo received recognition as one of the "model schools" in the state two years prior. Harjo boasted a state-of-the-art auditorium complete with an indoor basketball court. *The Record* reported that the facilities were modern enough for any town of 3,000 residents to be proud of. The building was a one-story brick facility with all concrete flooring and praised for being kept in a sanitary condition at all times. It included the most, "Splendid ventilation and natural lighting system." The teachers and the school district were even credited for Harjo's modern library.[2]

By 1929, the school was exploding with students, and the town was expected to experience exponential growth. This was more than the district or teachers had anticipated, and it was a problem no one was sure how to contend with. According to former students, however, the school's history was short-lived. In 1967, students and faculty were gathered, and with no prior notice, they were informed the district had decided to close the school. After forty years of service, families were now forced to make tough decisions: send children to the next district or forgo education altogether.

That was not the end of Harjo. Eventually, the school was purchased with the intent to repurpose the facility into a Christian school. However, challenges prevented reality from taking fruition. It was sold and then later reacquired by the current owner, whose parents had once dreamed of seeing Harjo a school again. While there is still intent to repurpose the grounds, it will more than likely never be an institution of learning. But the possibility is being explored that the building could be used in a fashion beneficial to the community. There is a possibility, for example, that Harjo could be converted into a farmer's market, a restaurant, or even a town community center.

## A History that Doesn't Exist

A new highway was built. Harjo plays Asher in basketball. St. Louis plays Harjo in baseball. Oil is booming! Small snippets in the *Tecumseh Oil Record* and mentionings of this or that. But nothing concrete. Even contact with the Oklahoma Historical Society failed to unearth any information about Harjo. Astonishingly information was nearly non-existent pertaining to the town's history or the school. Where did it come from? How was it funded? When exactly was it built? These were questions that frequently swam in the depths of my mind. However, as more stones were unturned, more questions presented themselves. How was there no history of this place?

Harjo is a Muscogee name, so I started with the Muscogee Nation to ask if there were any ties to the town. However, they did not have any record and could not offer any answers regarding the school or town's history. The next step was to contact the Citizen Potawatomi Nation. Harjo lies within Pottawatomie County boundaries, and I hoped that the Potawatomi might have some insight. While offering promising leads, the Citizen Potawatomi Nation indicated they too had no ties to Harjo.

The possibility exists that the Seminole Nation initially funded Harjo. The Citizen Potawatomi Nation indicated that during the 1920s, Harjo would have been within Seminole Nation territory. The Seminole Nation did not see this as being outside the realm of possibilities. While there was no direct knowledge of historical records, sources indicated that funding could have come from the tribe. School funding would have diminished as Seminole territory receded, and there was no longer any interest in sending Seminole Nation children to the facility. Eventually, the state would have supplied funds to allow the school to continue operations.

How does a town, and better yet, a school, fail to have any documented history? This is more common than one may realize. There are many reasons recorded history may not be available for a given town. First and foremost, history is local, and the locals are often the best source. History for a given location can be found in numerous places and curated in a variety of means. These can range from county records, historical society contributions, tax records, and state or town records. The size of a town may also be a factor in keeping records. In unfortunate circumstances, records may have been destroyed or not maintained.[3]

Harjo is considered an unincorporated community. According to the U.S. Census Bureau, these towns are often referred to as census-designated places (CDPs). These towns may closely resemble an incorporated town, but they lack many features such as some form of a functional government, elected officials, services, and lack a legally defined boundary. In many instances, these communities are privately

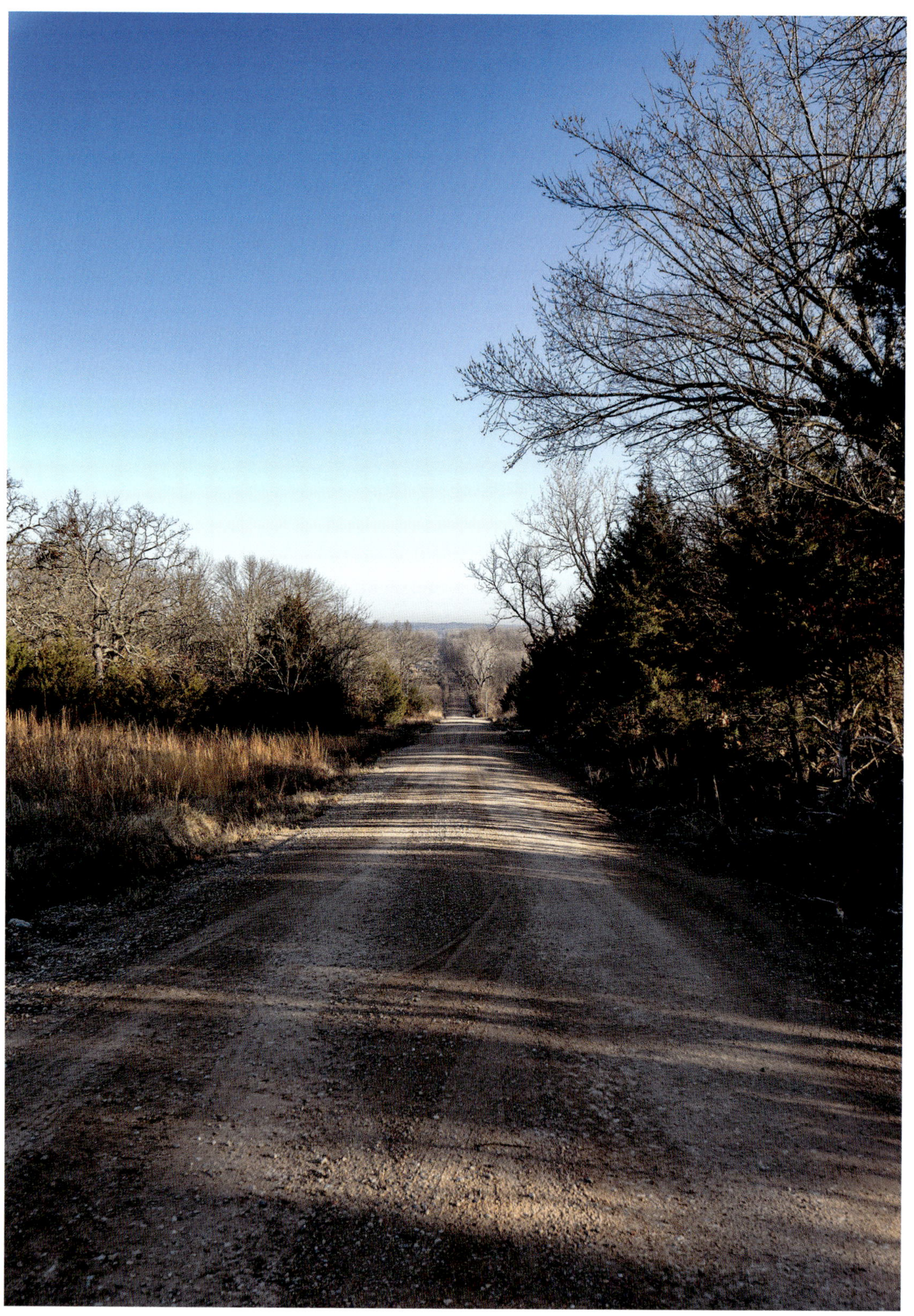

Backroads.

funded, and residents are responsible for securing utilities such as trash and water. They are often counted as part of the census.[4, 5]

Records indicate that Harjo had not participated in the 2010 census.[6] Population information was included with Maud, which is approximately 10 miles south and the closest neighboring incorporated town. This may also explain why little if any record is found regarding Harjo, and the town may have been considered an extension of Maud over the years. According to the school's current owner, the Maud public school system stores student records for Harjo Consolidated. No other official written record for Harjo appears to exist.

## Good Memories

A written record of personal reflection was located from a prior student. This is an excerpt of their memories.

> Harjo School was built and classes began in 1924. The school was a consolidation of Fairview, Tiner, Union, Mount Delonia and part of Pleasant Valley Districts to form the one Central High School. The first graduating class from Harjo was 1925. Harjo was rated one of the outstanding high schools in Pattawatomie [*sic*] County, according to scholastic standing, and basketball was the outstanding sport practiced in the school.
>
> A tornado heavily damaged the school on May 26, 1963. The entire roof of the main building had to be replaced or repaired due to wind and rain damage. The gymnasium had to be completely rebuilt and was done before basketball season that year. New flooring and ceiling had to be installed in the auditorium and a new stage built. New offices were built for the superintendent and principal on the south end of the auditorium and their old officers were converted to a library. Most of the school work was completed prior to the new school year.
>
> Harjo was a successful school for many years but due to the lack of the student body in 1967, the school closed. The last graduating class of 1967 consisted of 8 students. After the closing of Harjo School, many of their students came to Maud for the 1967–1968 school year, along with some of the employees.

# 3

# THESE HALLOWED HALLS

The allure of this institution is indescribable, but often is the case with old schools. One tends to form an intimate relationship with the facility that can be as marrow-deep as it is for those who once attended. There are memories here, and hearing stories from prior students solidifies that lives were molded by this place. For those of us who were privileged enough to have attended modern facilities that are not in danger of closing, we take for granted the meaning these institutions behold for former students, faculty, and staff.

Harjo has been vandalized over the years, but more of the damage is the result of time. While there is hope that the institution will be functional again, there is a race against the elements. Most of the damage and decay can be attributed to a lack of use and upkeep. The foundation is primarily sturdy, and many of the outer walls appear in good condition. However, the roof has sustained significant damage over time. Nature is reclaiming the grounds.

I am just as enamored with the history of these majestic buildings as much as I am in the beauty of their current state of decay, but a sense of melancholy often sets in. There is more than finding art in these decaying structures. They are filled with memories and a sense of when life seemed a little less confusing to some.

Harjo is dying, and in more ways than one. Just as with so many other institutions before it and the many more to come, it will fade with time should no one repurpose the building. But it is not just the decay that is taking its toll on Harjo. Small towns in Oklahoma and all over the U.S. have very little, if any, written history. What little recorded exists is often shared through oral history. That is until the last soul with ties to a given facility or town passes on. What history is known about Harjo lies with its alumni and a few local residents. But their numbers are dwindling as the years pass.

And with time, even if the building remains, Harjo's history will be lost to the ages.

I met with the Harjo Alumni Association's vice president, who was gracious enough to describe their experiences. I even received a guided tour of the facility. Approximately seventy alumni attend annual reunions; a number not too shabby for a school that closed over fifty years ago. Reunions are held in the nearby town of Maud. However, as the years pass, this dedicated body of a pioneer institution will fade into oblivion. Harjo has become an institution of lore. Oral history is what keeps the memory of this place alive.

I developed a vision of what each room would have been used for when I first walked the halls of Harjo. Most of my perceptions were a reflection of how my childhood schools looked. I guessed at each room. This one looks like the main office; that one, maybe a classroom. However, even my best guesses were wrong.

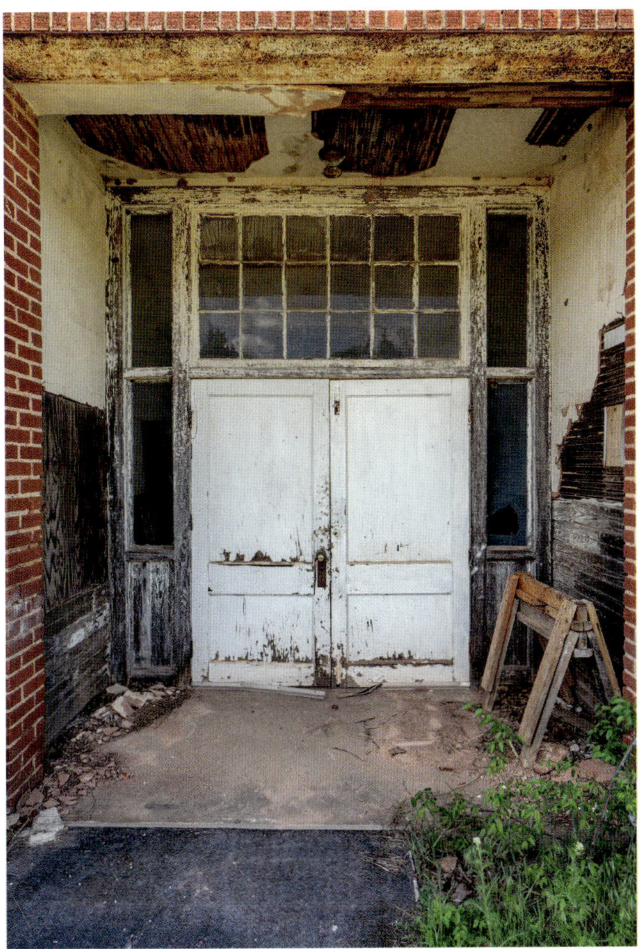

Harjo's main entrance.

Harjo was an intuition that housed first-grade through high school-level students. However, the primary focus was educating first through eighth grade. High school students were often interlaced with other classrooms. They patiently waited until teachers finished delivering their lessons to younger students before shifting focus to the high schoolers.

There are four entrances: two that face east, one to the south, and one to the west. The front entrance is marked with the school's name. "Consolidated Dist. No. 5," it reads. The main hallway is long and would have appeared to stretch out to eternity if I were a young student. Six doors line the hallway (three on each side), and each color-coded. However, it was unclear whether the color-coding was an original concept or an implementation after the school's closure.

The current owners were in the process of reorganizing. An array of items found temporary residence in either the hallway or in a classroom. Rooms were divided based on their intended purpose. On the left (south) side of the building were classrooms; on the right (north), rooms for various purposes.

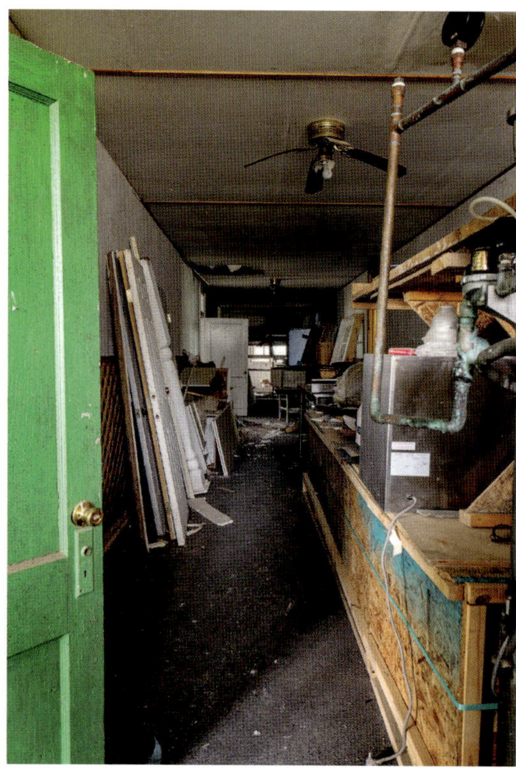

Harjo's main hallway looking west.

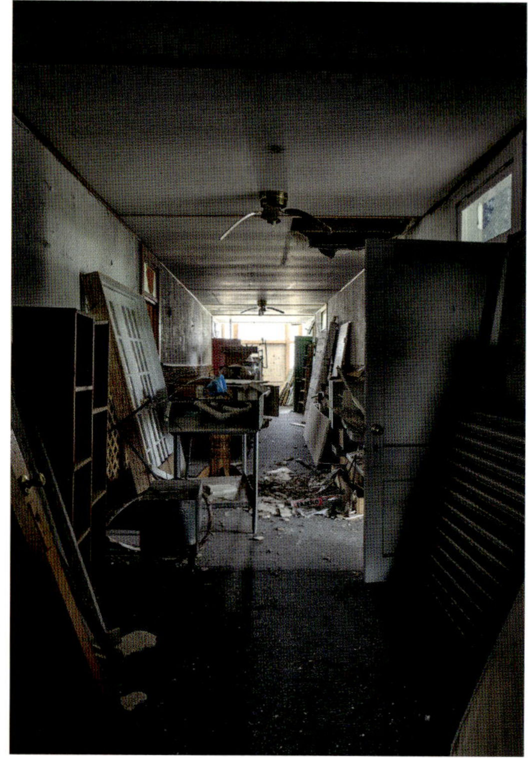

Harjo's main hallway looking east towards the main entrance.

# The Northern Rooms

## THE MUSIC ROOM

The first room to the north was the old music room and in better shape than all others. The 1960s décor still remains the same as it was when the facility closed. Now, it is vacant save for being used as storage. Aside from a few broken windows, the room remains in good condition, all things considered. Nothing indicates that this would ever have been a classroom.

My guide relished fond memories of watching world series games from 1961–1964 in this room. Most notable was witnessing the New York Yankees battle it out with the L.A. Dodgers in 1963. Many of the greats played. Don Drysdale and Sandy Koufax for the Dodgers. Names like Mikey Mantle, Whitey Ford, and Roger Maris graced the Yankees.

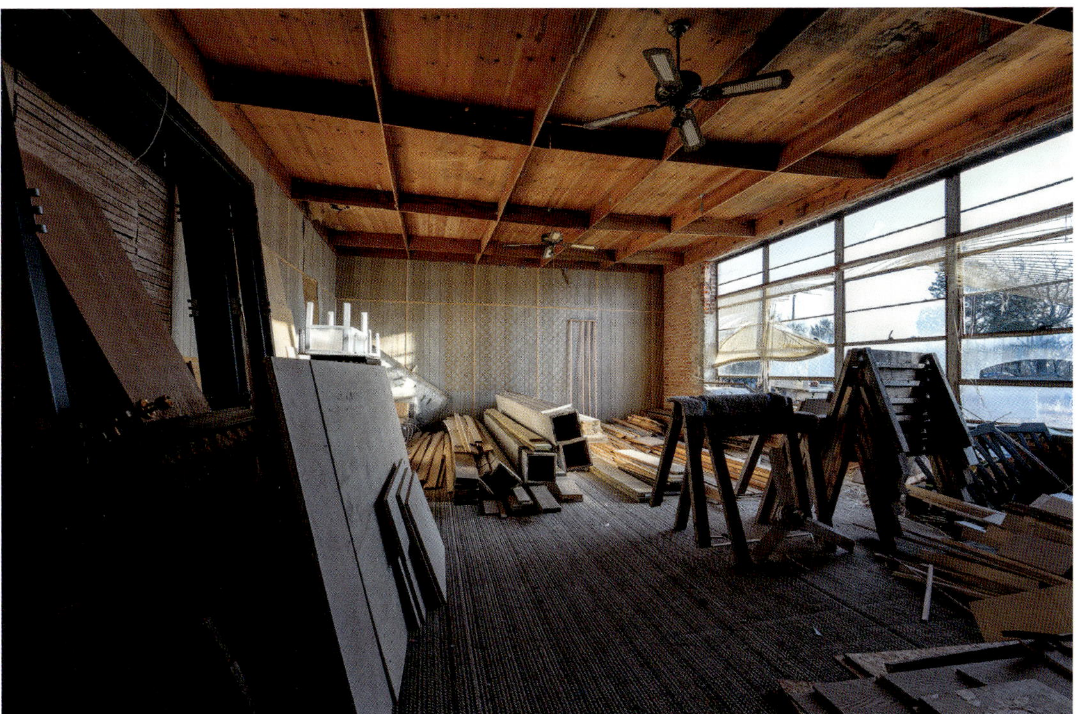

The music room.

## STORAGE AND PLAY AREAS

The middle room was used as a playroom, which was later converted to a storage room. A mixture of carpet and wood planking covers the floor. It was hard to imagine how pristine the woodwork may have been when the school was in its prime. Several holes are in the ceiling from the years of water damage, rot, and decay. This room, like the others, has a unique smell. Bedding, debris, building supplies, and personal effects line the floors. Faux wood paneling, especially popular in many Oklahoman homes, still line the walls.

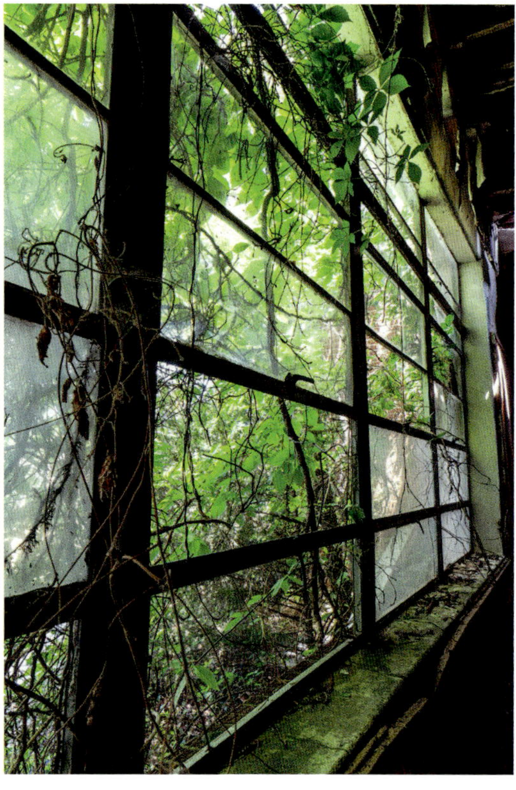

The playroom windows are overgrown with vegetation.

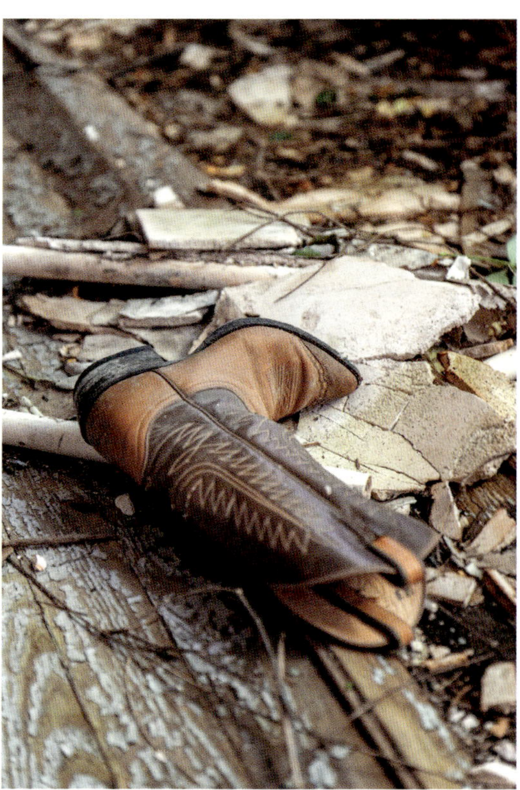

Random personal effects on the playroom floor.

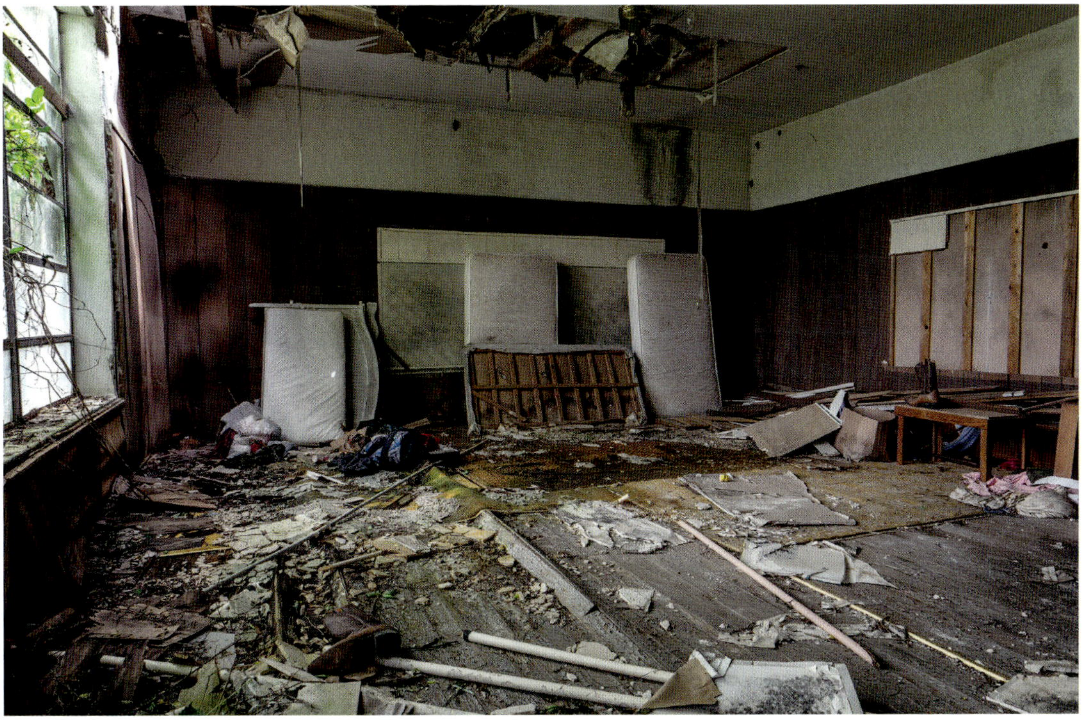

The playroom floor buckles after years of exposure to the elements.

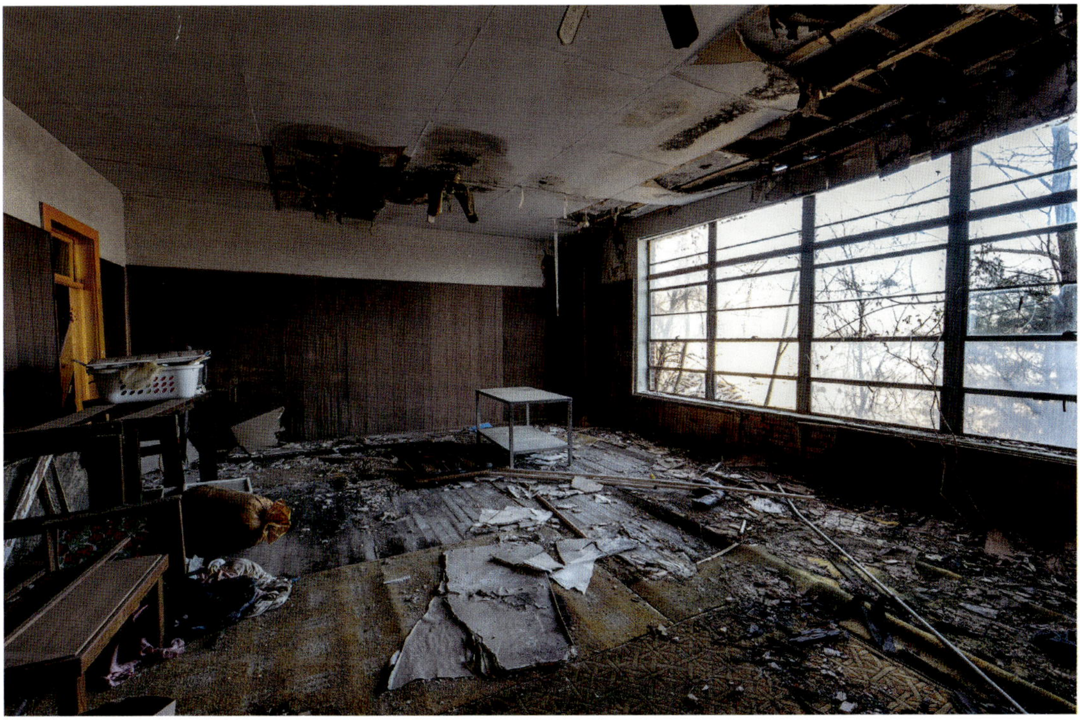

Vegetation recedes in the winter months.

## THE LIBRARY

The library is the last north-facing room, and it is showing signs of its age. Debris from the overhead ceiling is strewn about the floor. The water-stained carpet was most likely original. Walls are laced with mold, and the room smells of mildew more than other rooms. I noticed that each room has a distinct scent, which is undoubtedly due to the varying amounts of decay in each location. It was as if each room could be identified by its odor rather than the color of its door.

The floor has a spongy feel in spots. While the foundation is concrete, it was hard to discern what was creating the uneasy feeling that I could fall through at any moment. An air condition unit was in the room, but it is safe to assume that it was not an original fixture.

This room once belonged to the superintendent and principal before their offices were moved to the back of the auditorium. The *Tecumseh Oil Record* describes the library in all its splendor; however, this raises the question as to whether this was the original library or where it was eventually moved to. The latter is the more likely scenario. The room was also used to teach the high school students.

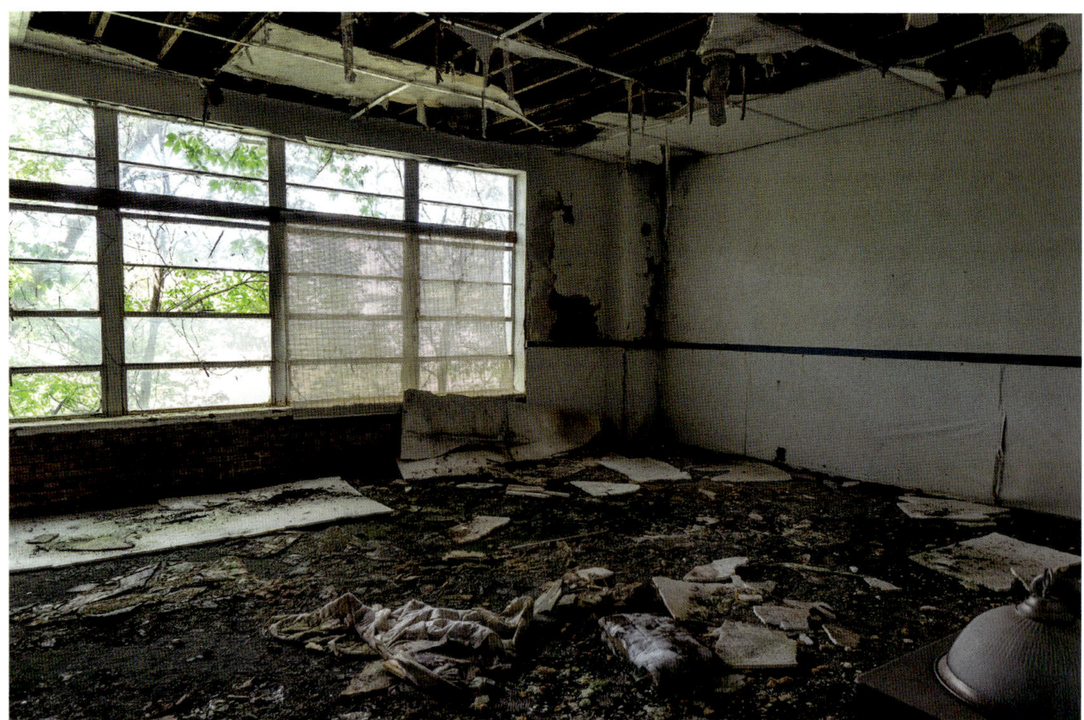

Mold, mildew, and decay have taken over the former library.

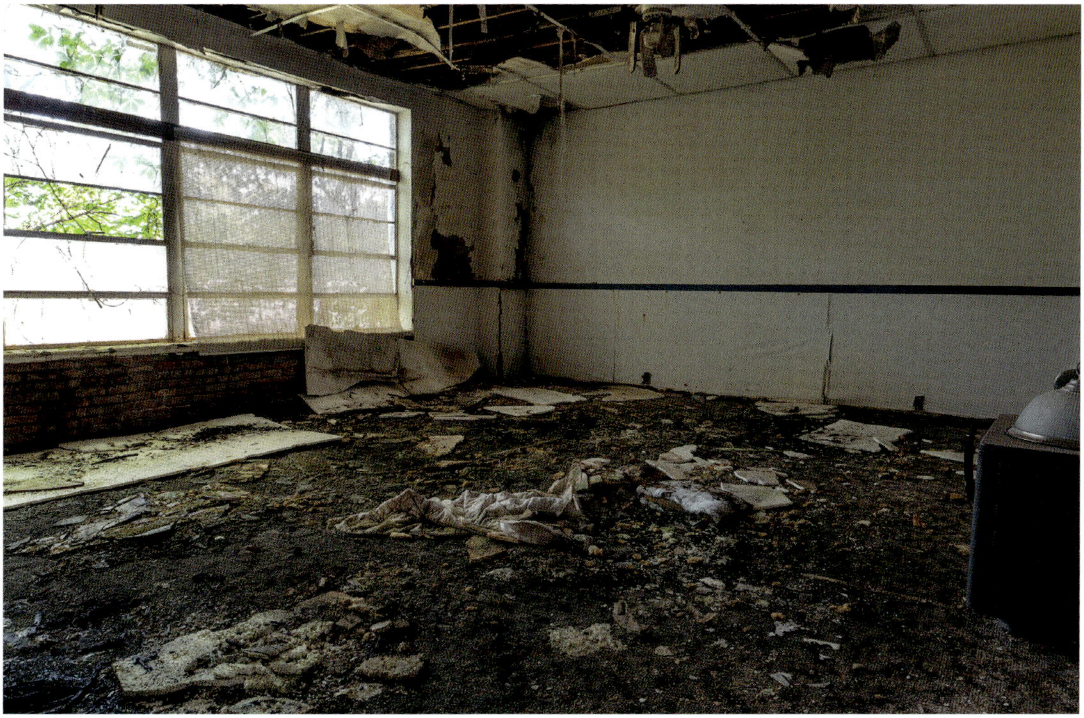

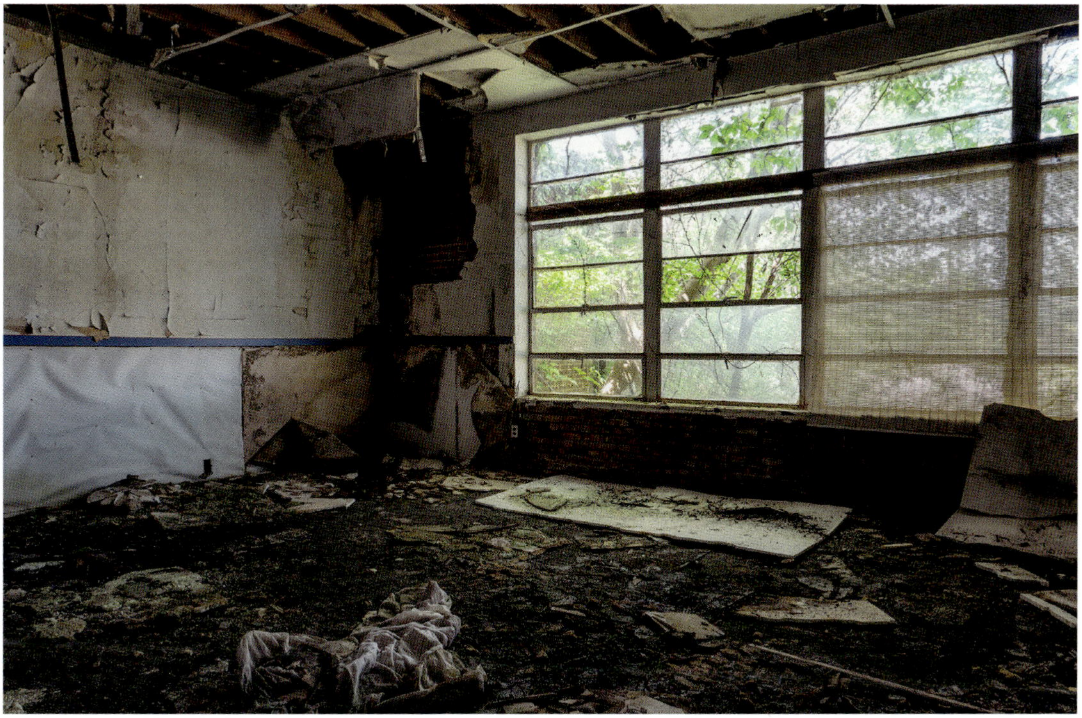

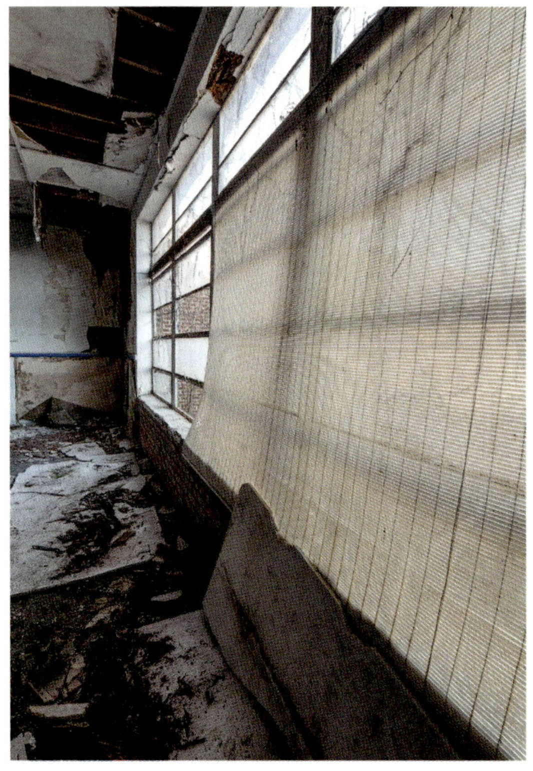

The west library wall has crumbled more in prior months, demonstrating how fast Harjo is decaying.

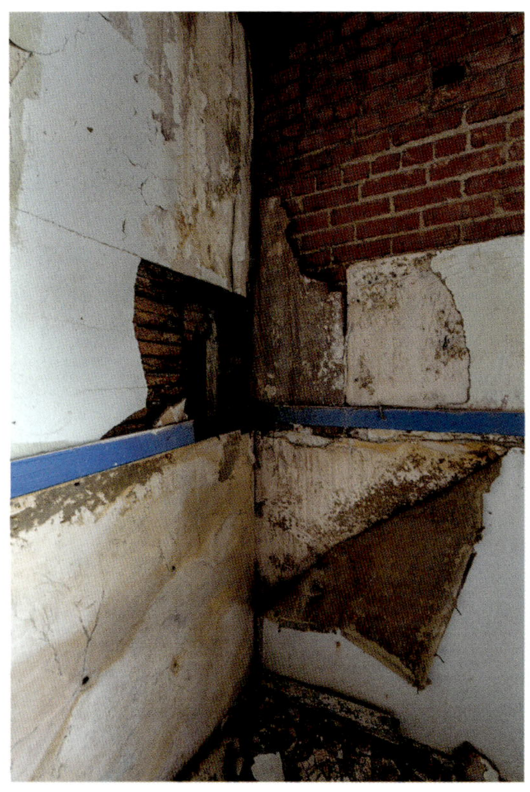

## SOUTHERN ROOMS

Classrooms are located on the south side of the main hallway. Each classroom housed a range of grades: (1) third through fifth and first through second, respectively; (2) sixth through eighth; and (3) high school.

### GRADES ONE THROUGH FIVE

The first two southern rooms have the appearance that they could have been the main office at one time. In fact, the main office would have made logical sense. It is a spacious room located by the main entrance. But the room held third through fifth-grade and first through second-grade, respectively. The rooms are now joined, but at one time, they would have been separated. The roof and ceiling are falling down in spots. It is most likely the second best room in the facility in terms of condition. Now, it is used as storage.

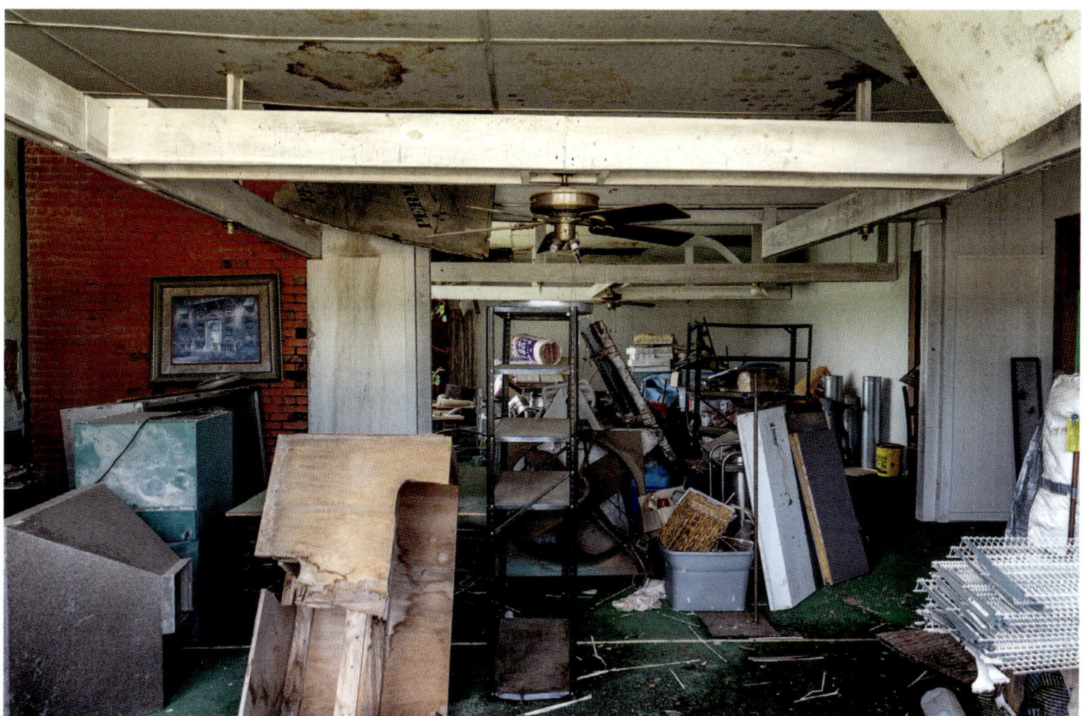

First through fifth-grade classrooms now joined.

## GRADES SIX THROUGH EIGHT

The last room on the south side of the building held sixth through eighth-graders. Like other rooms, the damage is extensive. Light protrudes from various openings in the roof. Many of the windows have been broken, and various forms of vegetation now find their way in. Mold and mildew have a strong presence. A trophy case is located in the back of the room. An old couch sits in the middle of the room.

Each time I visit an abandoned building, I find myself wondering if a given item was an original fixture or if it was placed there. Sometimes one of the surprisingly exciting parts about abandoned exploration is revisiting a facility to see what has changed. Often objects are moved, randomly seem to appear out of nowhere, or are destroyed. In this instance, older pictures of the room seem to indicate the couch most likely had been there for some time.

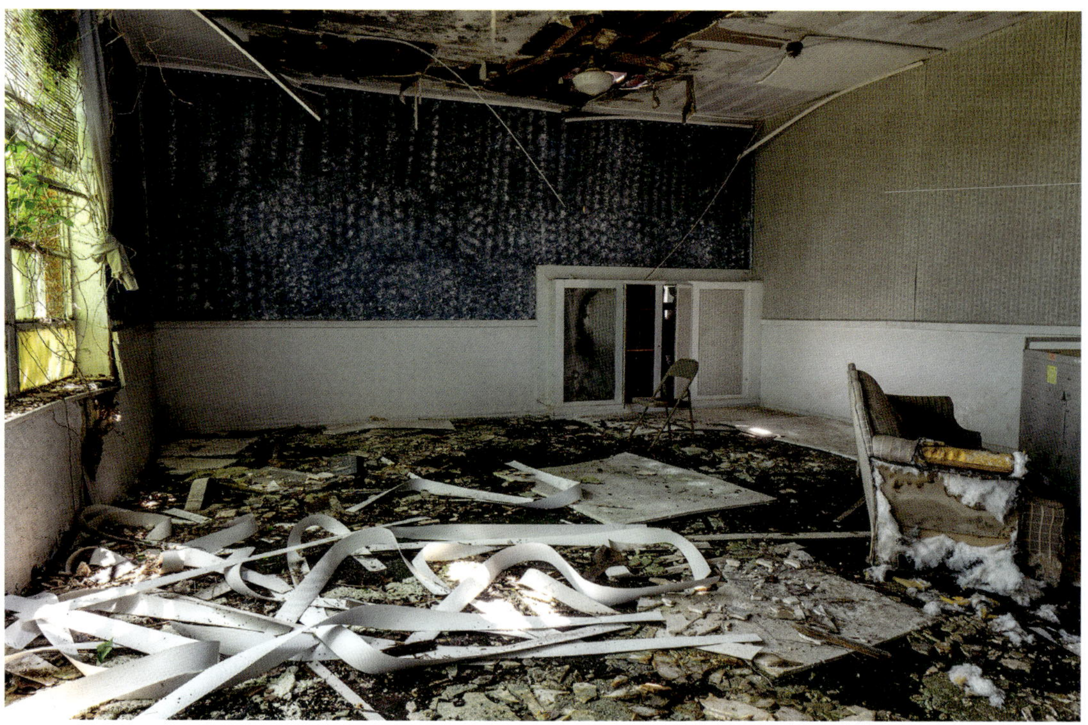

The debris-laden sixth through eighth-grade classroom. Access to the school trophy case is located in the back corner.

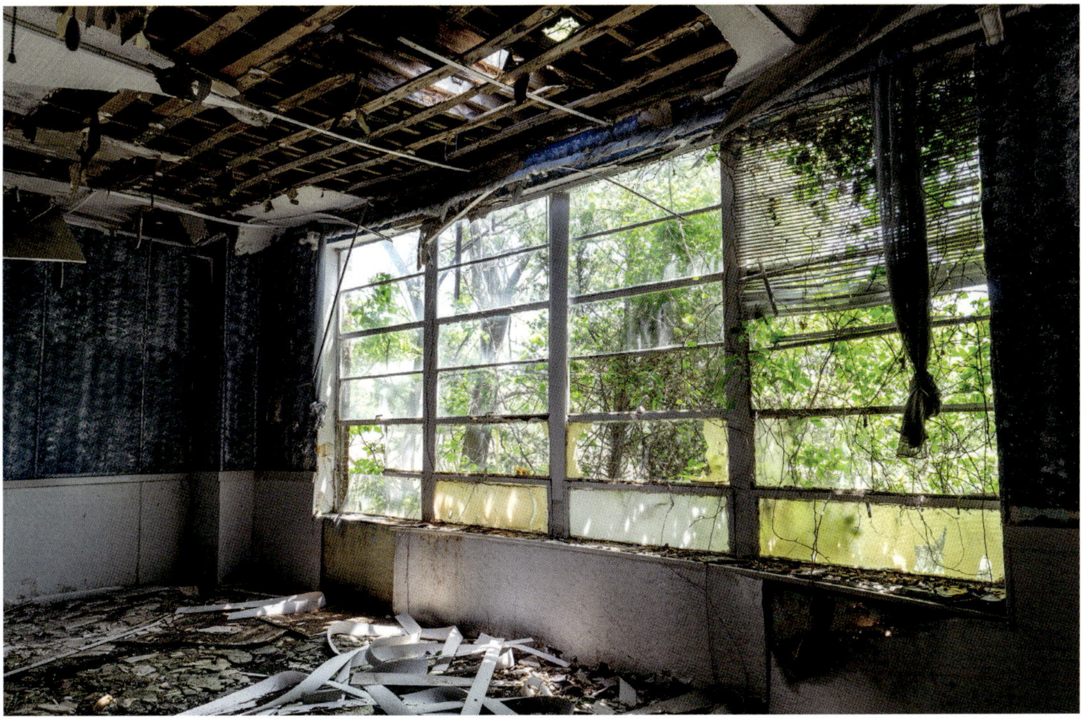

*Above:* Most of the ceiling is missing, and the room is exposed to the elements.

*Right:* A drape still hangs.

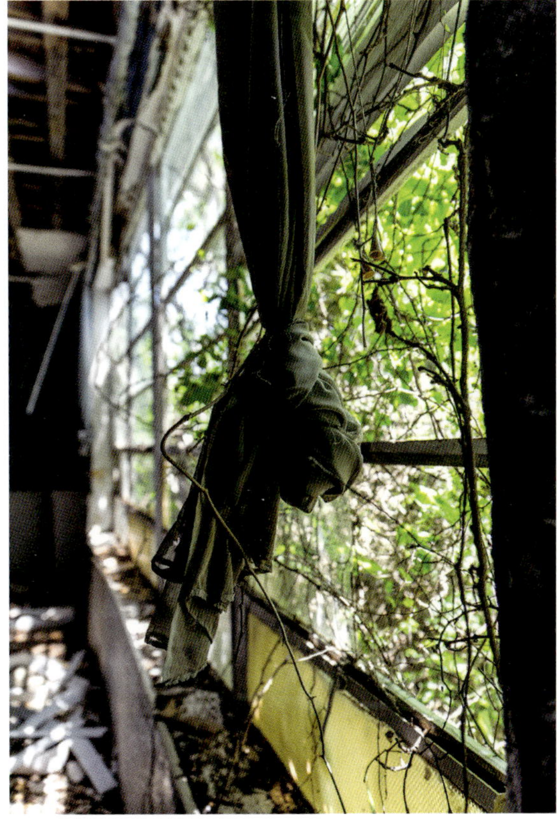

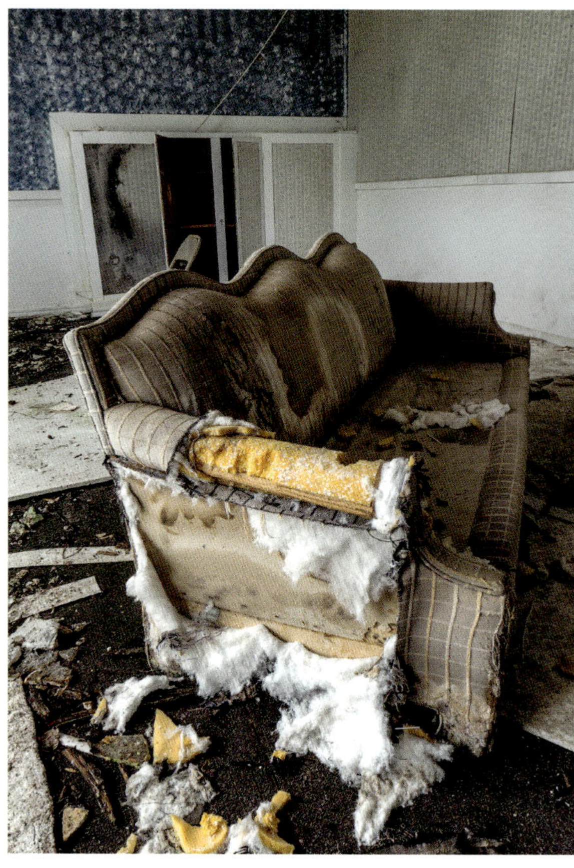

Old furniture is still scattered throughout the facility.

## THE STAIRS

Conditions of the building worsen as one presses deeper. At the end of the main hallway lies a small flight of stairs. This is one of two points in the building where there is a slight change in elevation. At the base of the stairs is a hallway that leads to the south entrance. On my first visit, the south entrance was boarded, but modest amounts of light peered through. Paneling has since been removed during recent renovations.

This secondary entrance leads to the south lawn. The school trophy case is to the left (or students' right as they entered), which is accessible from the sixth through the eighth-grade class. The south lawn served as a playground. However, it was also a drop-off point for parents and school busses. At one point, a bus barn was also located in this area. Former students referred to the south entrance as the main entrance to the school because it was used most frequently, even though that was not the official designation.

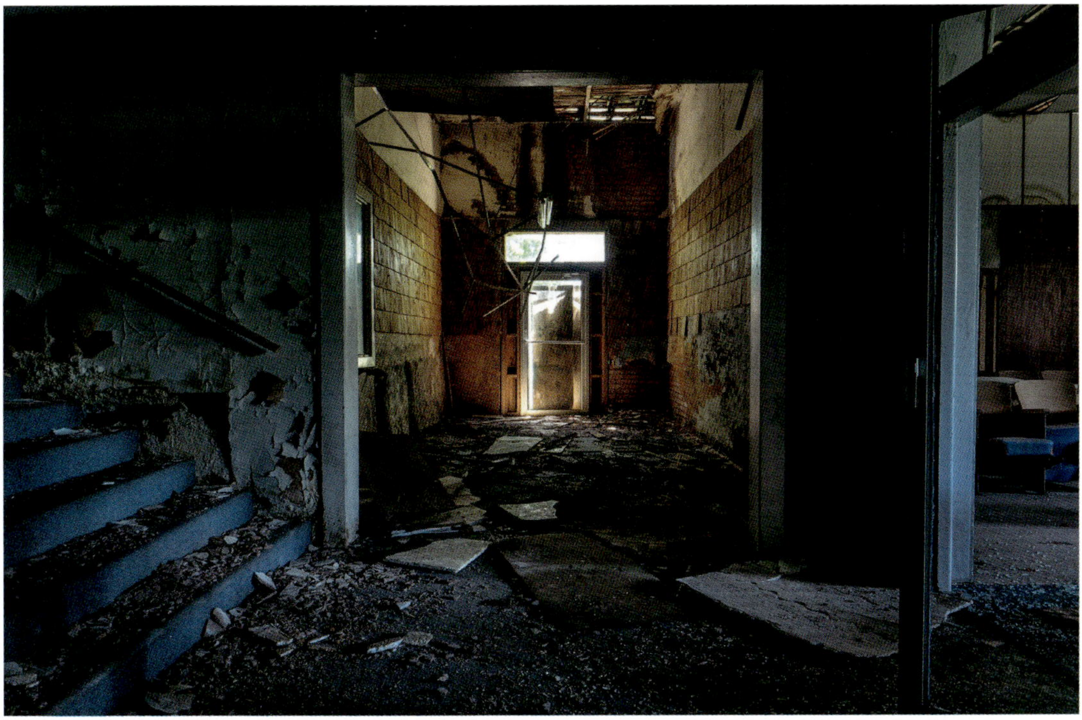

Harjo's south entrance and staircase.

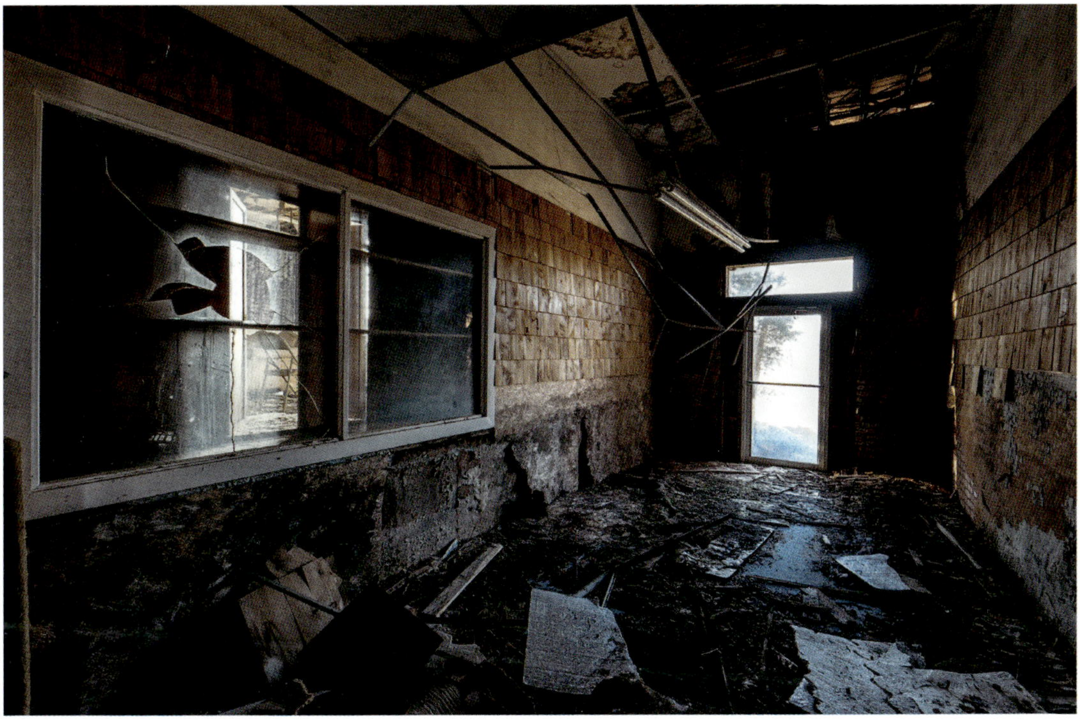

Harjo's trophy case and south entrance. Boards previously covering the south entrance have been removed during recent renovations.

## THE AMERICAN TEACHERAGE

Early in Harjo's history, the south lawn included housing for the principal and superintendent. However, one of the prominent features was the teacherage. Teachers were known to move frequently in the late 1800s. This resulted in the need to board them at each location. Some towns provided boarding facilities for teachers, while others would board at homes of students. This resulted in often less than ideal conditions for everyone.[1]

According to an article in *The Journal of General Education*, while the practice of boarding teachers was common, it was far from ideal. Teachers often complained about the lack of privacy, area to study, poor food, and quarters far too small to support an extended-stay guest. Residents were also not too fond of the practice. Often boarding a teacher meant an added burden to a family, which also encroached on their privacy.[2]

School districts began to consolidate in the late 1890s. As with Harjo, many institutions began bussing in students from multiple rural and farming communities. To meet the demand of educating the masses, school districts found it necessary to employ better-trained teachers and administrative staff who would remain a more permanent fixture to the institution. However, with this requirement came demands from professionals by way of better pay and living arrangements. The teacherage was the solution.[3]

Teacherages were housing that was provided by the school district. These living quarters resolved many of the concerns and complaints expressed by teachers and

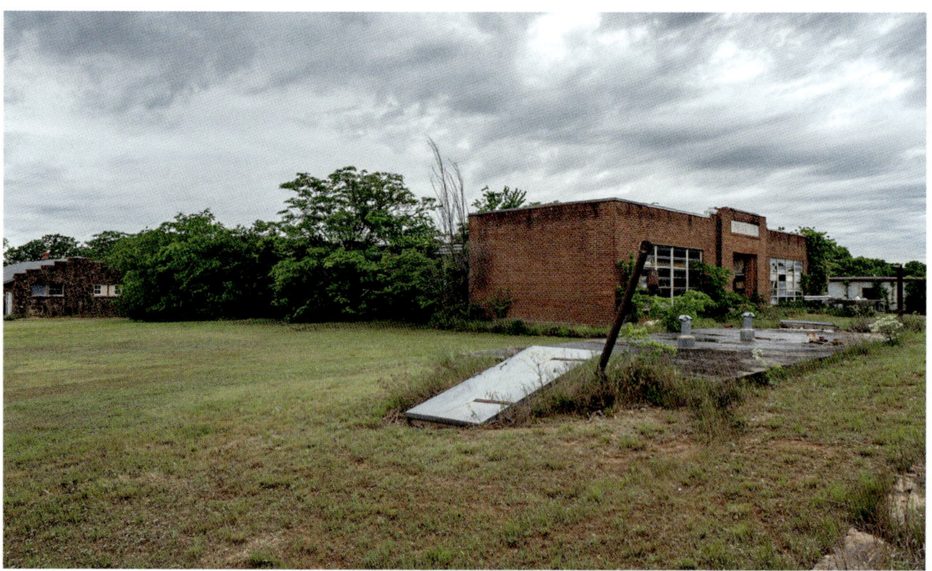

Harjo's south lawn and storm cellar. At one time, this area would have been used as a turnaround. Teacherages and administrative housing were also located on the south lawn.

families. It also offered a level of stability, which afforded teachers the ability to be more of a contributing member within a given community. Teacherages could range anywhere from individual housing to residency halls with multiple levels and living units.[4]

## THE AUDITORIUM

Evidence of the roof's demise becomes more prominent in the auditorium. Located at the end of the staircase and attached to the main building, the auditorium was reported to be one of the most prolific designs of its time. Now it is a dank and silent mausoleum to former memories. The roof over this area is far worse than any other in the building. Extensive water damage is evident. However, auditorium seating is mostly intact. A medium blue carpet covers the old basketball flooring, which buckles from years of water damage and neglect. In the back of the auditorium are the remains of the superintendent and principal's offices.

At a recent school reunion, a former student shared a story of when he and fellow classmates laid new flooring. They removed the old planks that ran the room's width and replaced it with a narrow oak plank that ran the auditorium's length. However, after sharing recent pictures, a former student confirmed that someone had replaced the floor he helped lay. It once again runs the width of the room. The conclusion was that the floor was changed at some point after Harjo closed.

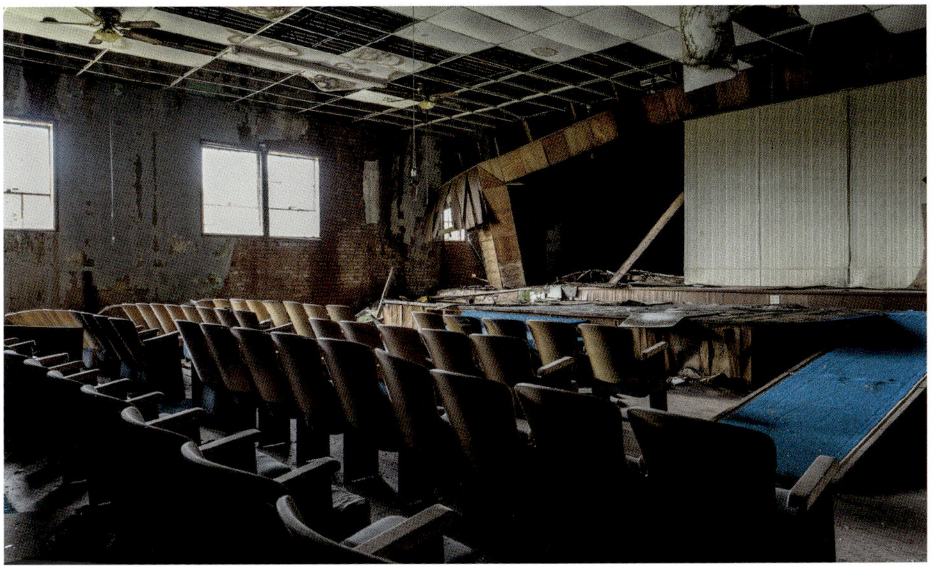

Harjo's auditorium. Blue carpet covers old basketball flooring. The stage has seen better days.

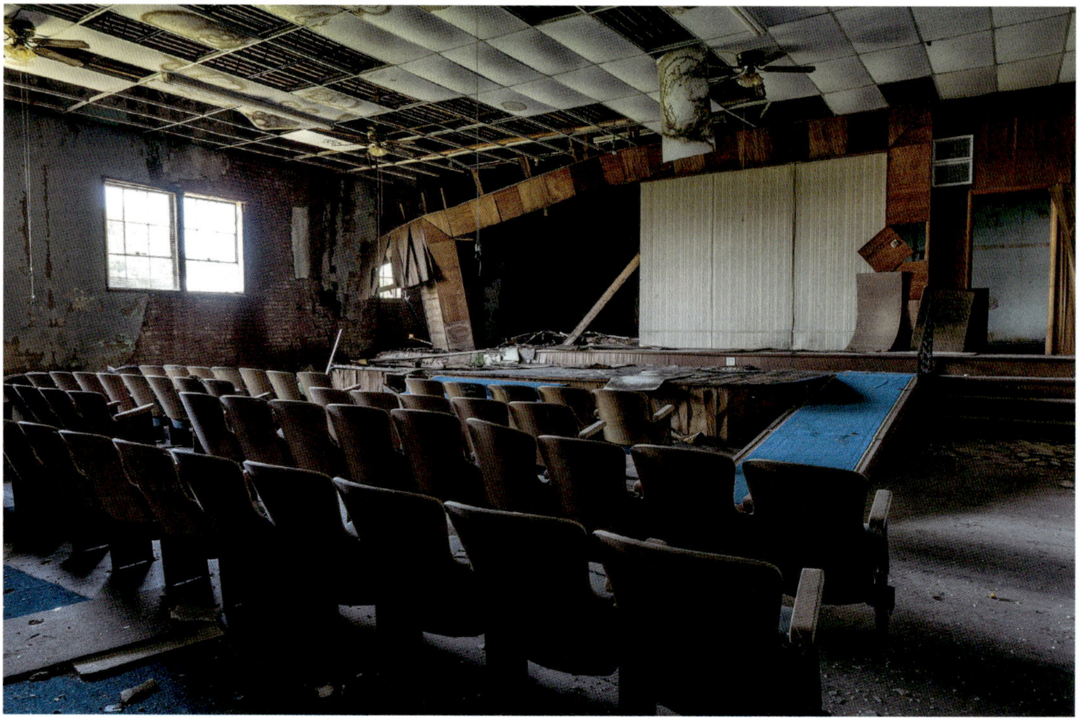

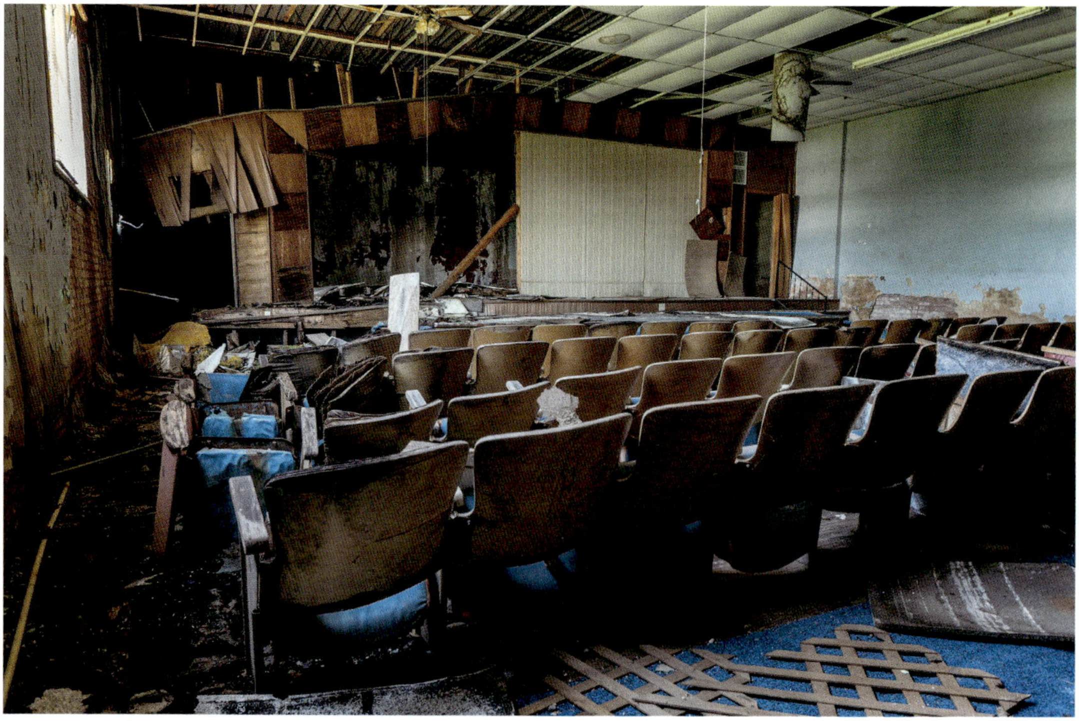

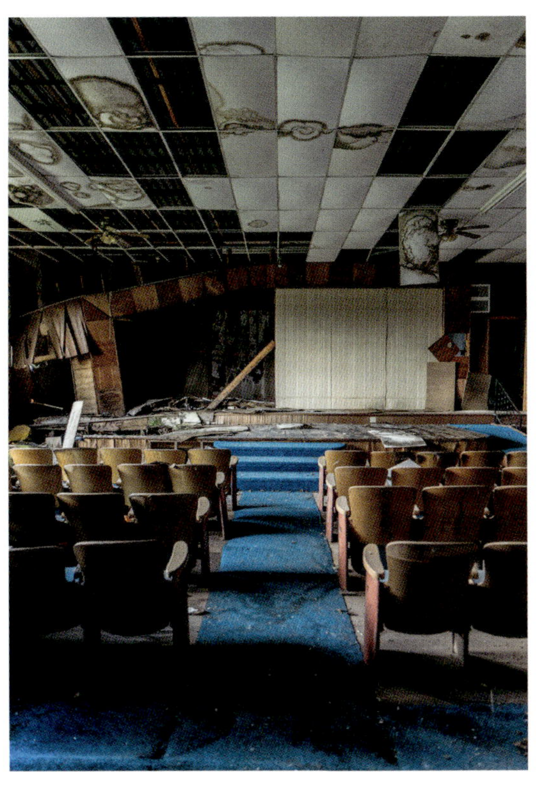

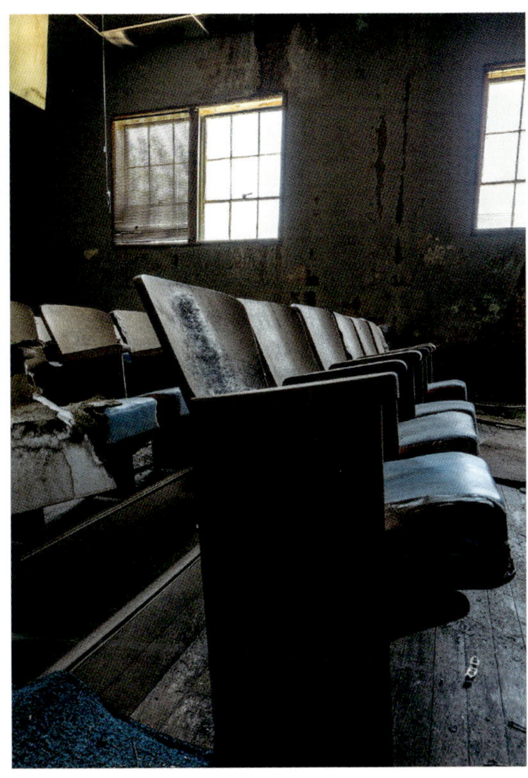

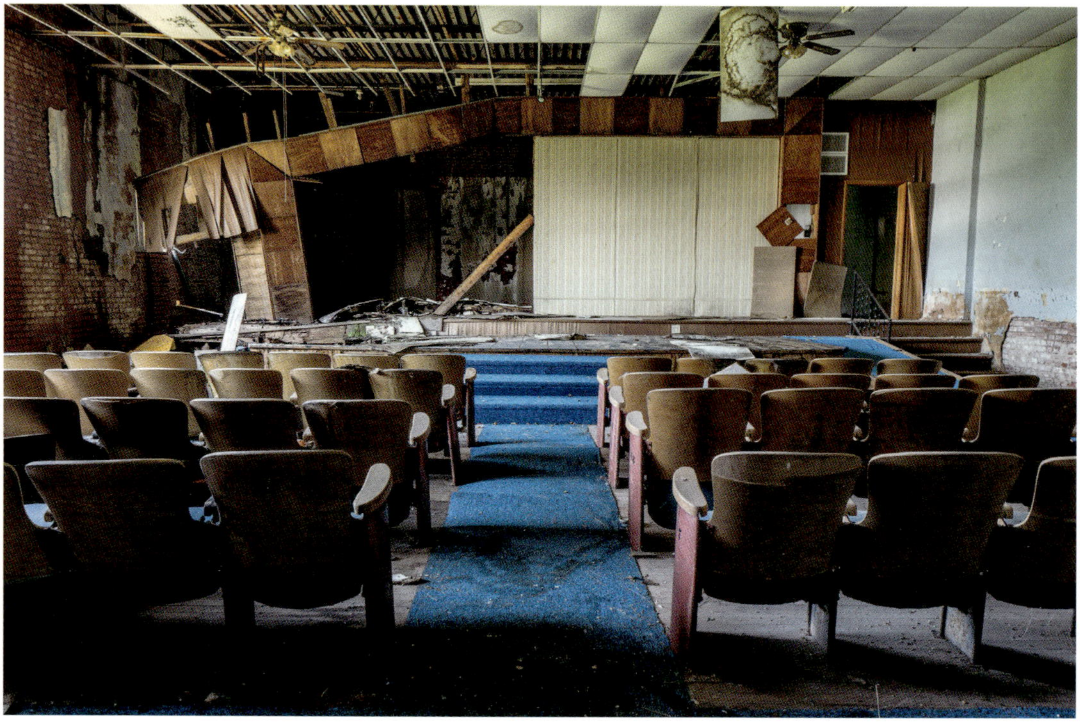

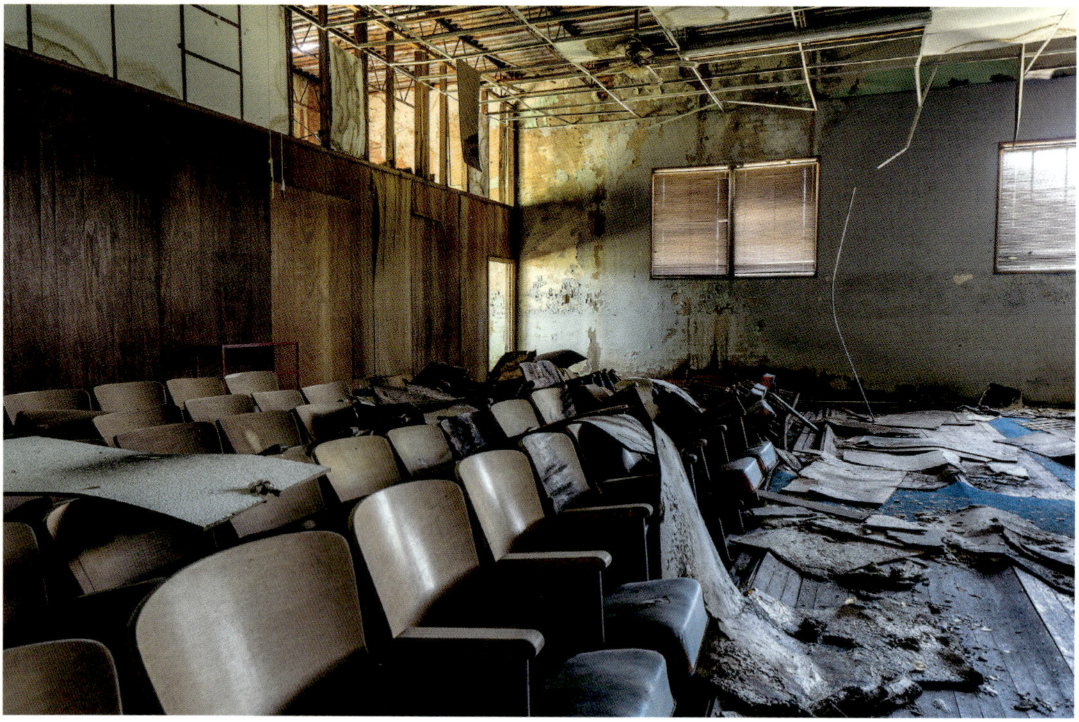

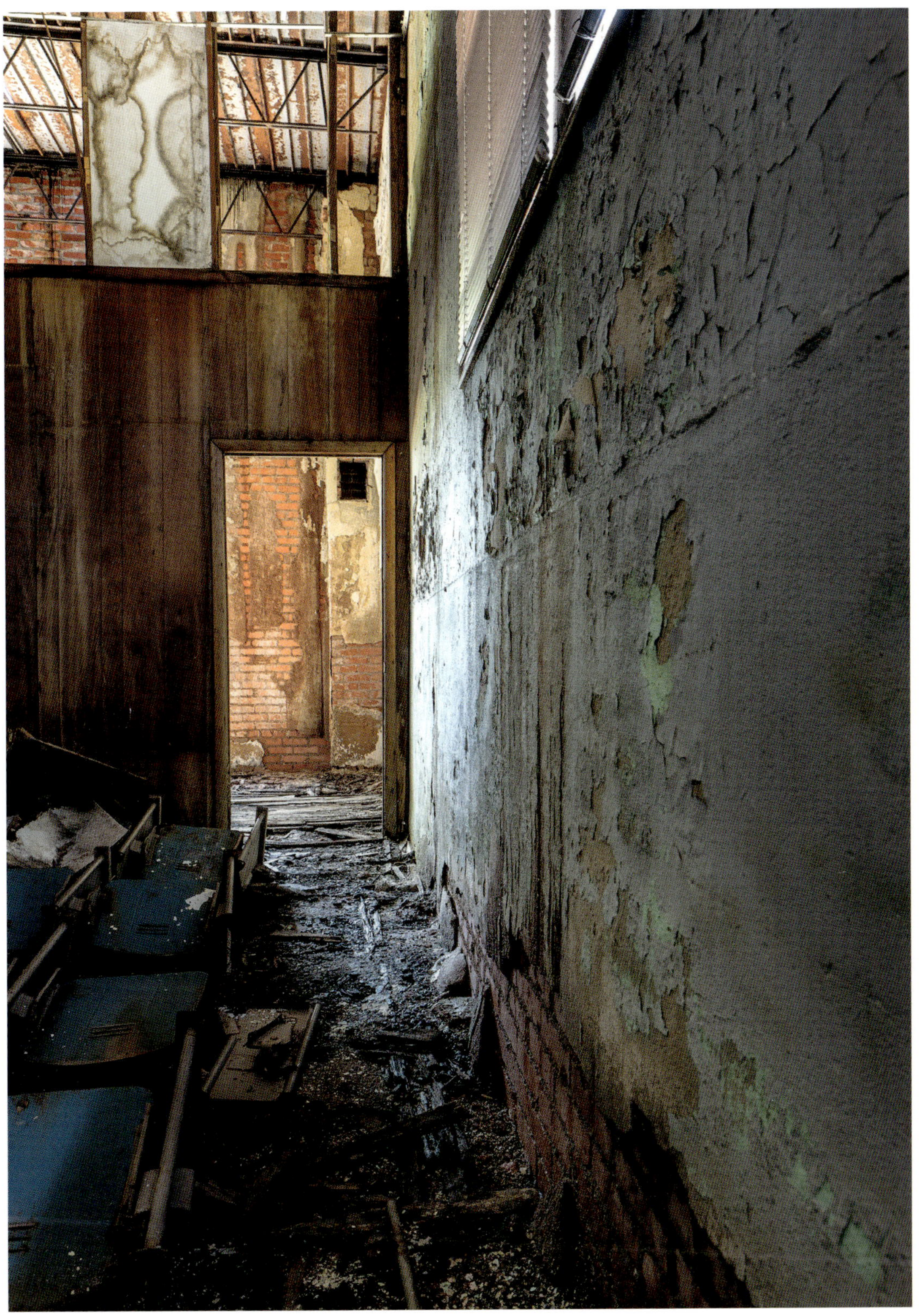

The west wall of the auditorium leading to the south offices.

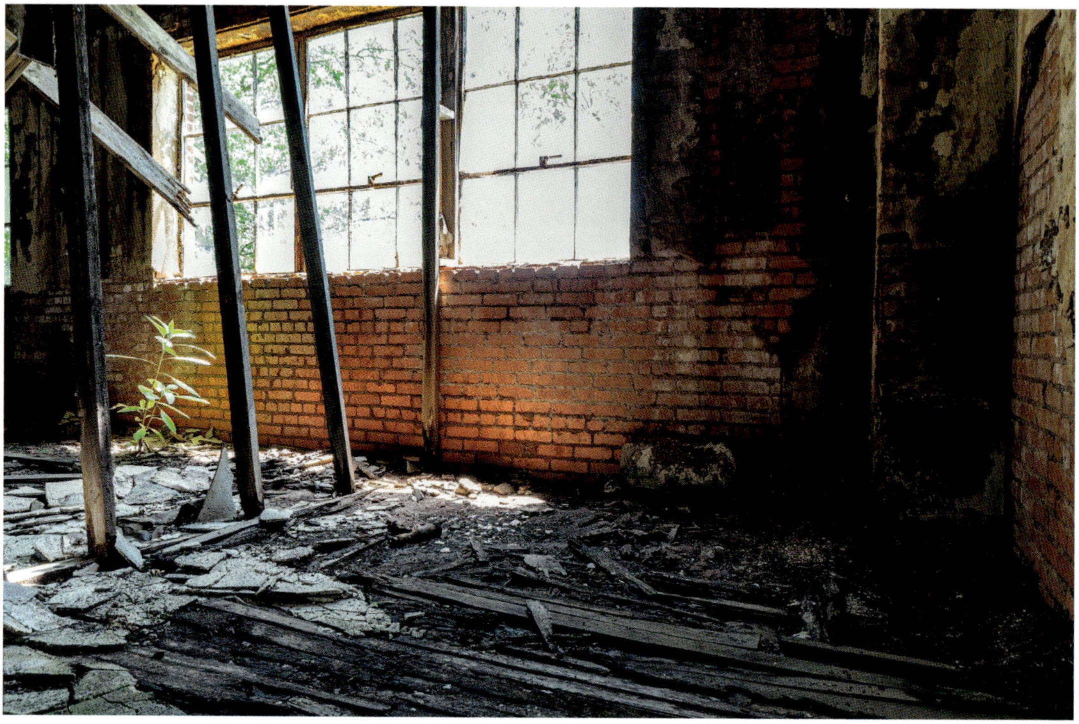

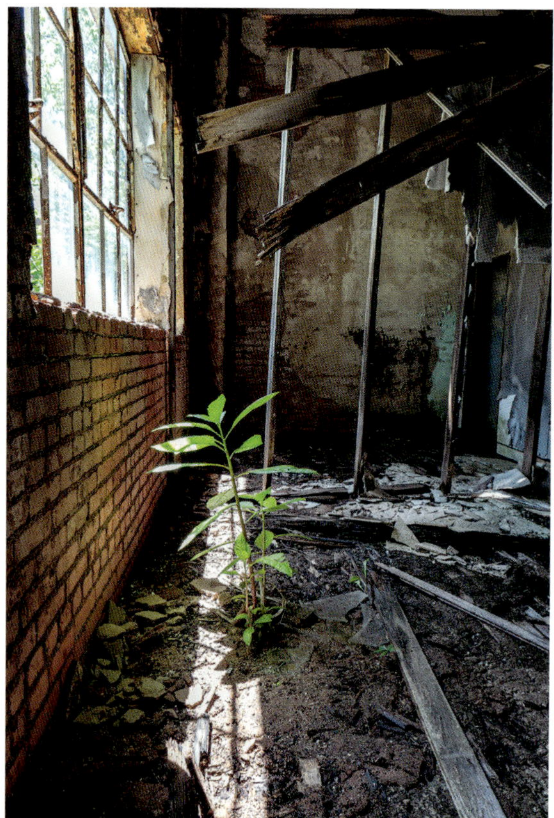

Life has found a way. The south area of the auditorium was converted to offices for the principal and superintendent.

Another former student shared memories of the venue, which included school assemblies. He noted that the auditorium was also used as a gym, but that the ceilings were too low for him to understand how basketball could have been played here. The *Tecumseh Oil Record* also described the modern auditorium, which included basketball nets.

I have a fascination with stages. There is something magical about them, and the allure brings back memories of excitement and curiosity as a child. The stage was one of life's coveted curiosities that only select classmates had the privilege of exploring and being able to see what resides behind the curtain. While some of Harjo's stage remains intact, it is far from safe. The main ramp and stairs appeared sturdy, but most of the structure was far too degraded to safely support anyone now. A behind-the-scenes look shows how badly the structure has collapsed. A large gaping hole consumes a majority of the stage, though the immensity of its size is indiscernible from the front.

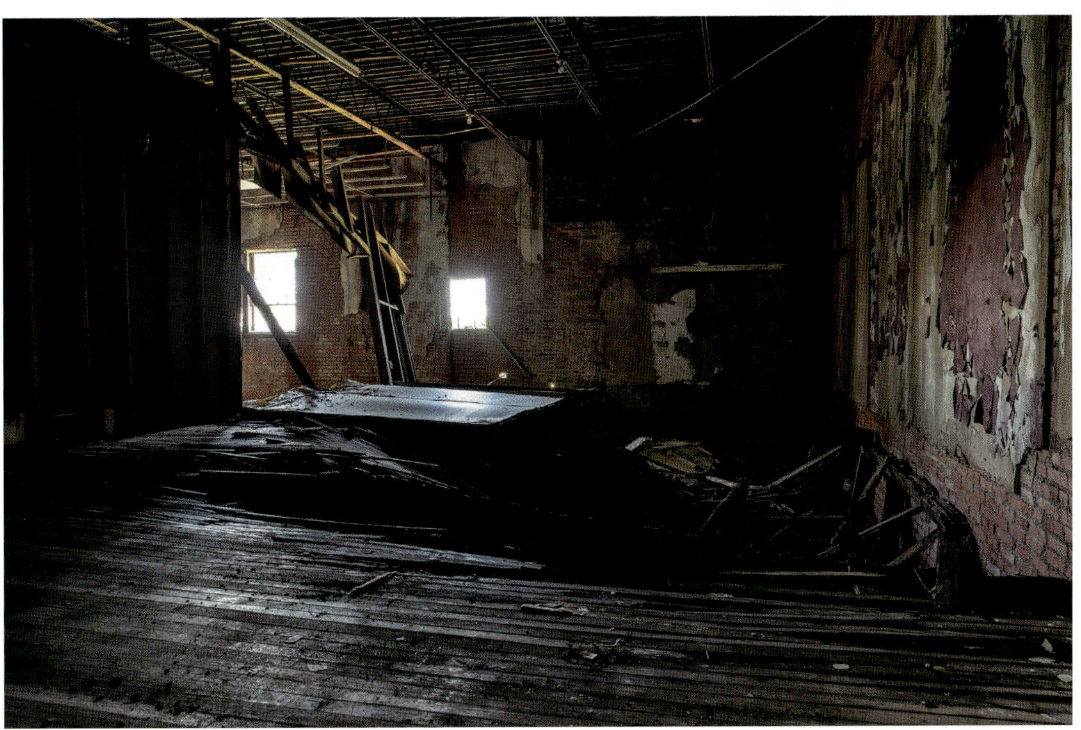

Extensive damage and a gaping hole in the auditorium stage.

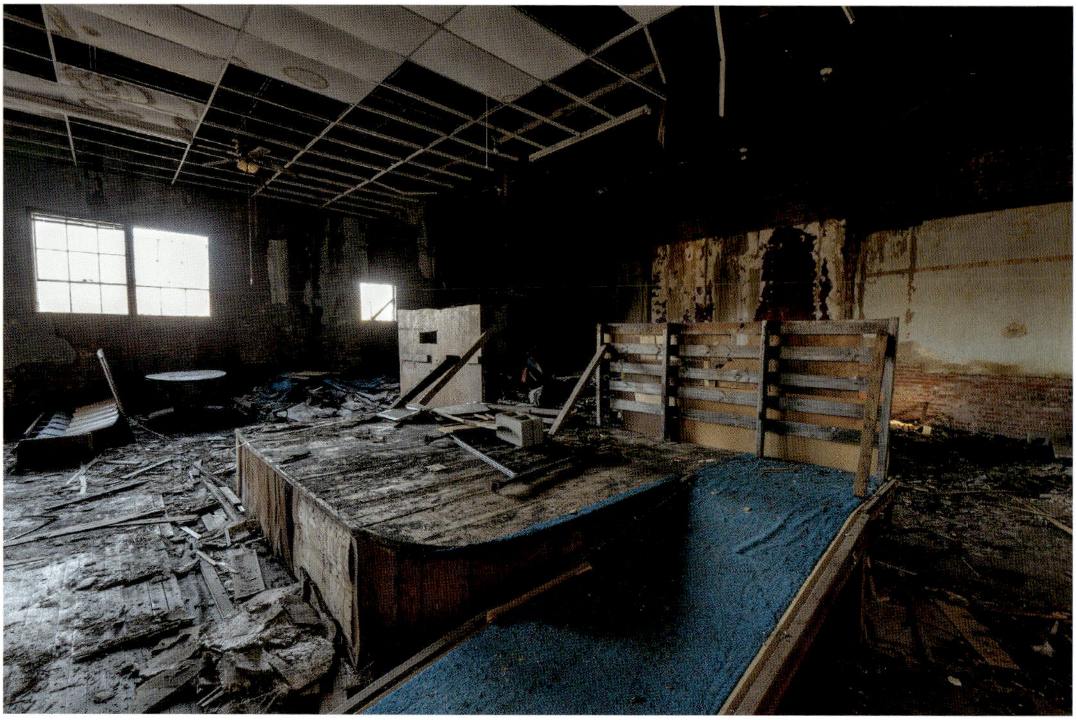

Renovation work continues, and the auditorium is slowly being dismantled. The stage is now all but gone.

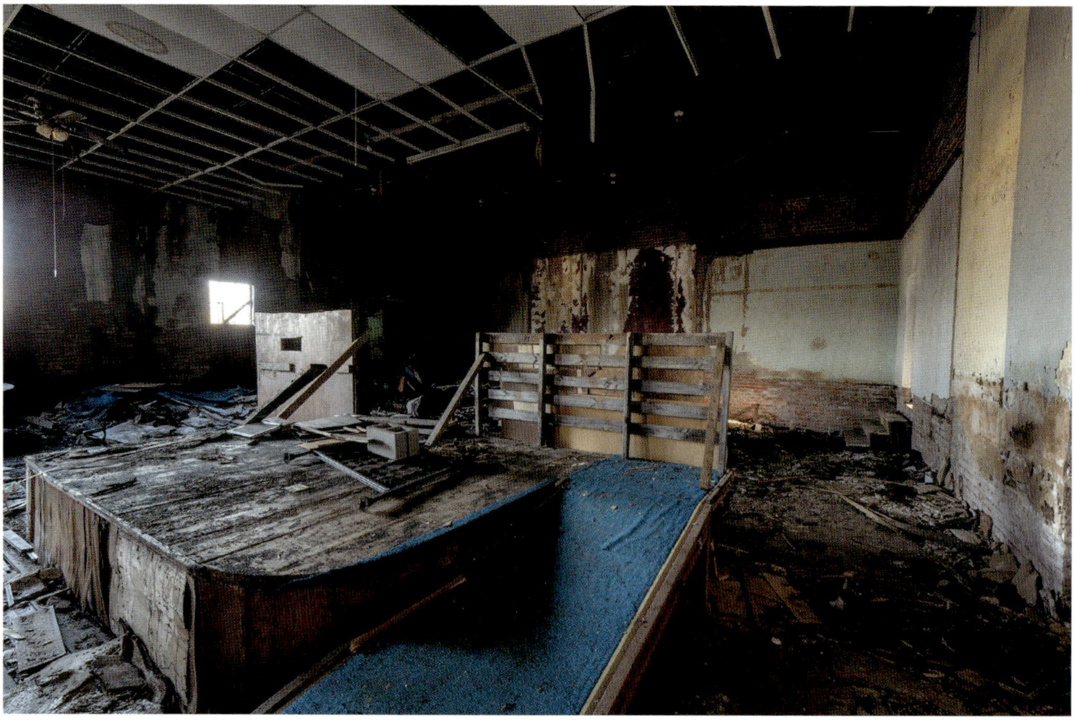

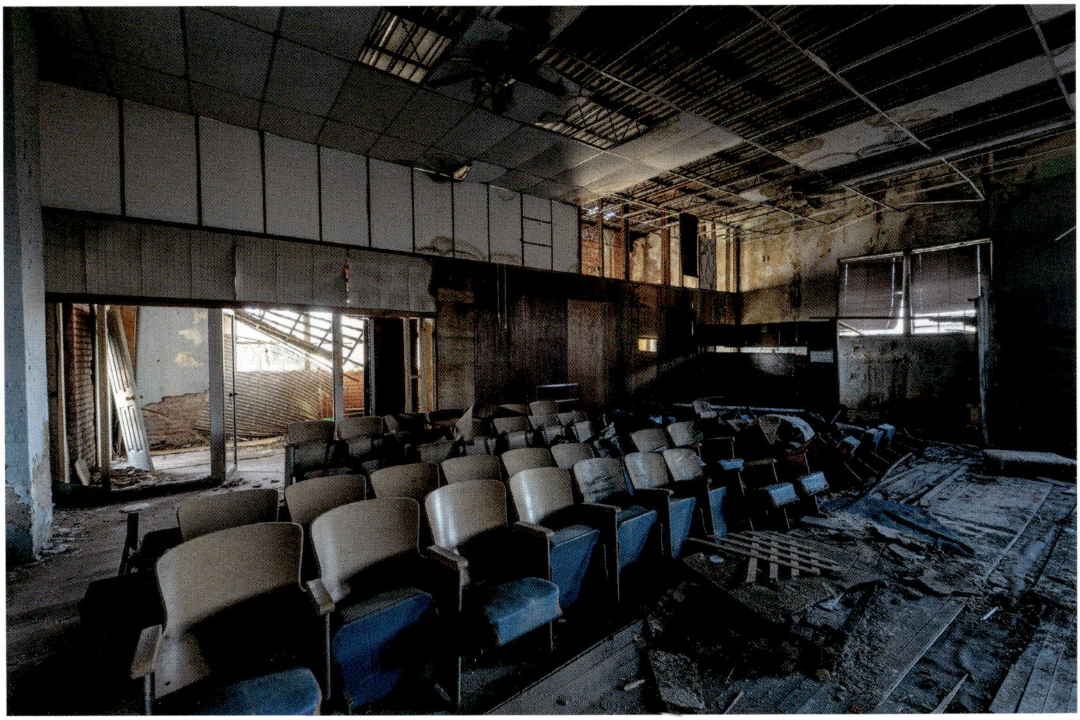

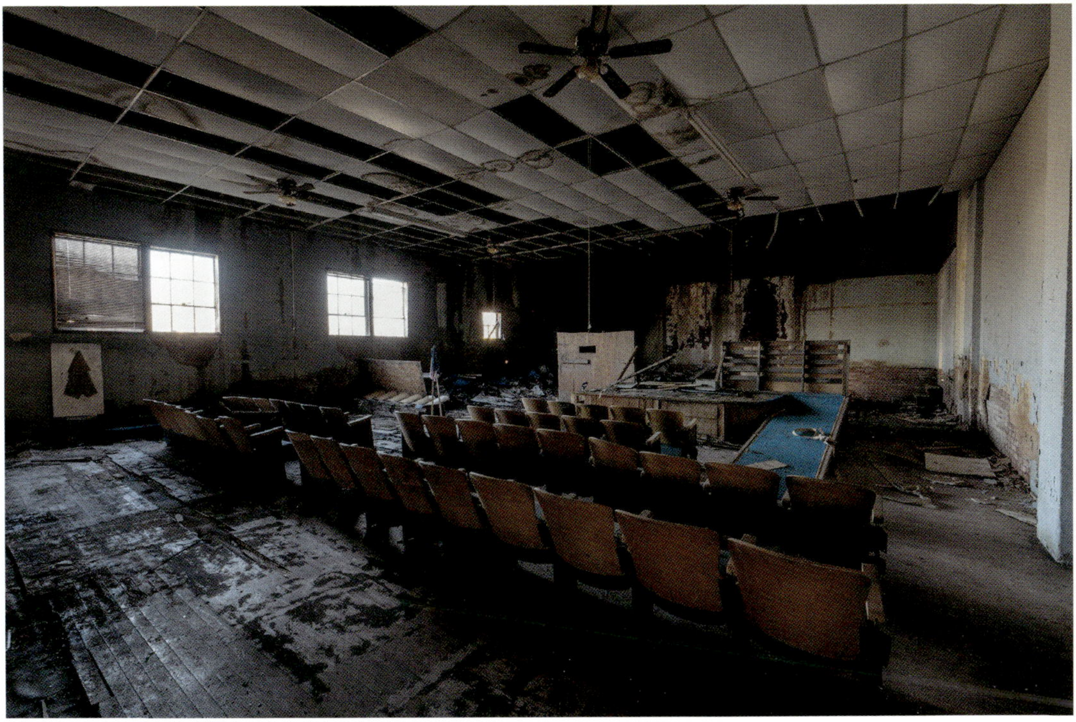

## THE FINAL WALK

I continued to snake along the z-shaped hallways and traversed past the backstage area. Abeam the backstage stairs is the third entrance that faces east. While there is no longer a door, the entryway is almost completely hidden during summer months when ivy encapsulates the building.

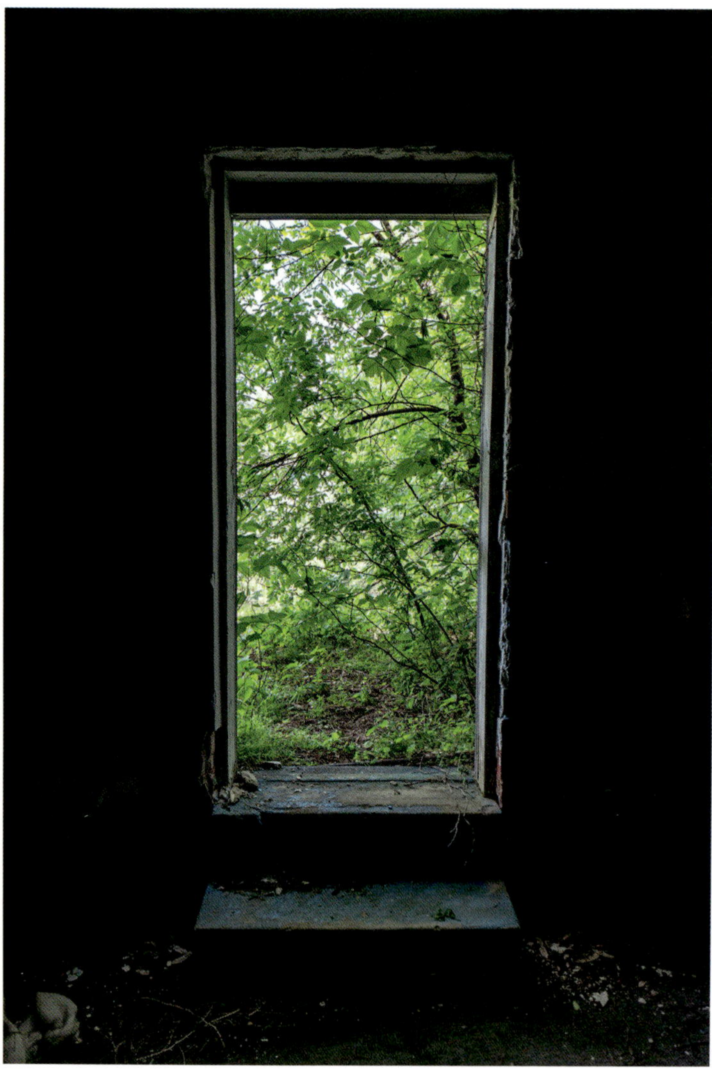

Harjo's east-facing entrance. In the summer months, it is safely hidden by vegetation.

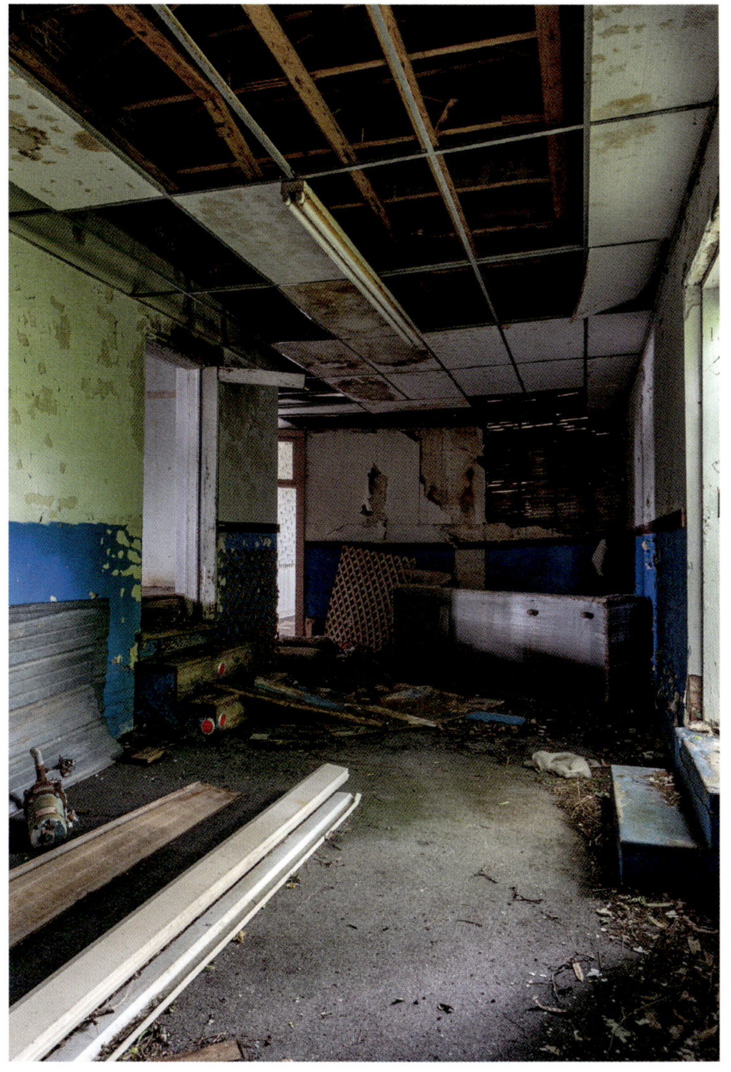

The north hallway. On the left is the entrance to the backstage. The east entrance is to the right.

The hallway turns back once again to the west completing the z-shaped pattern. Another couch and random sorts scatter the hall. Three rooms are in this area. The first was an old room that has since been retrofitted with shelving—a byproduct of one of the prior owners who used the facility as a bible school. It was also one of the rooms in far worse shape than the other two in this area, and it once served as the driver's ed and typing classroom. Next to that, the main office. The room is plain and barren with little flare or appeal compared to the other rooms.

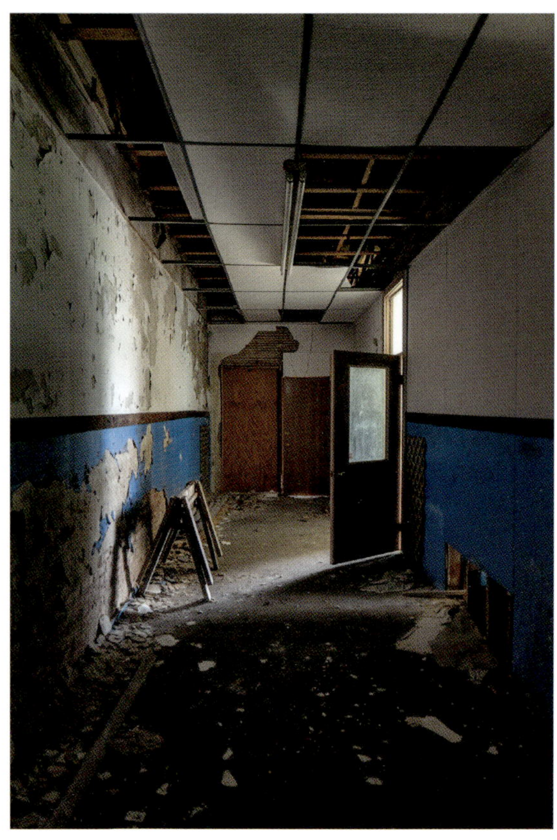

Completing the Z. The short east and west running hallway is located in the northern portion of the building.

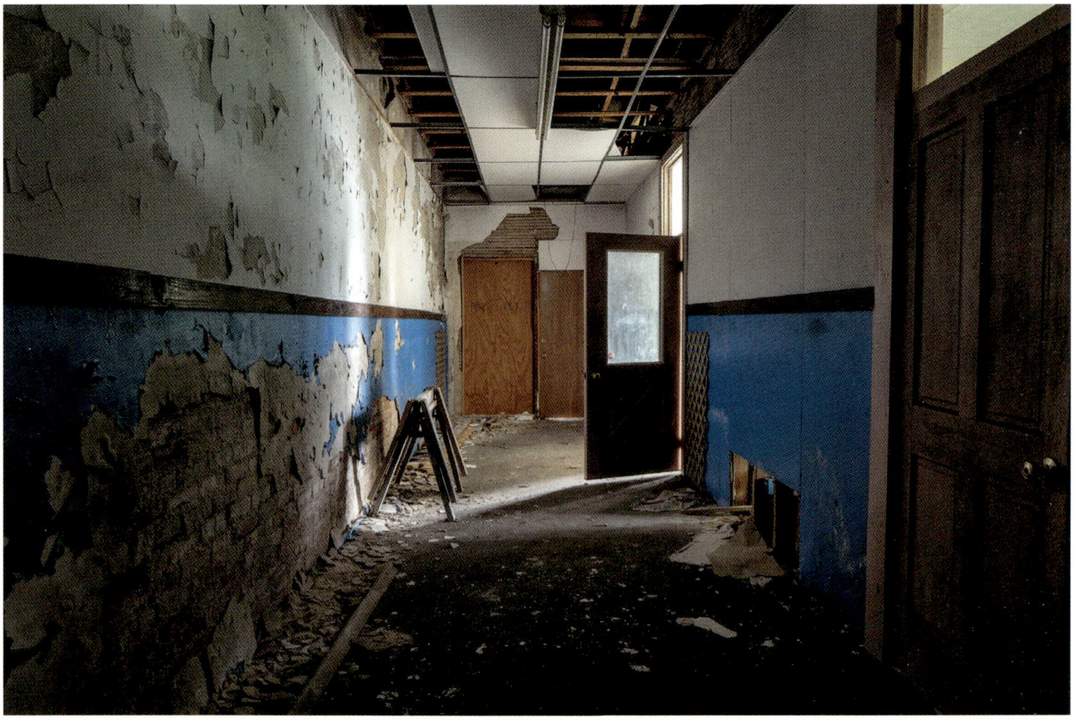

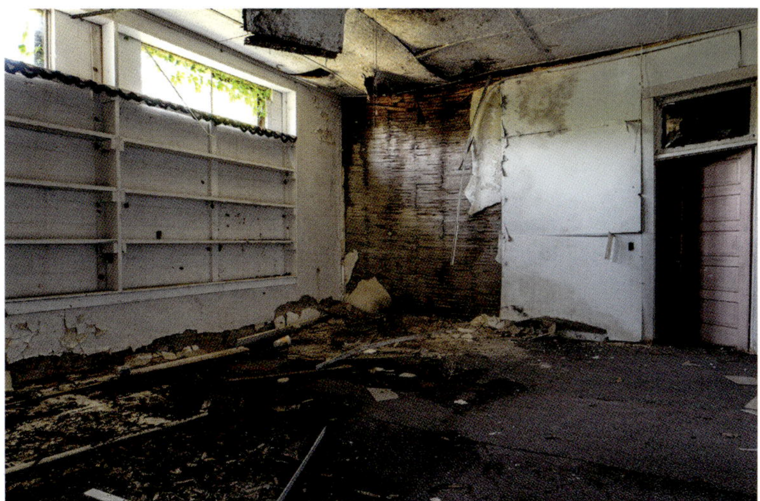

The former driver's education and typing room.

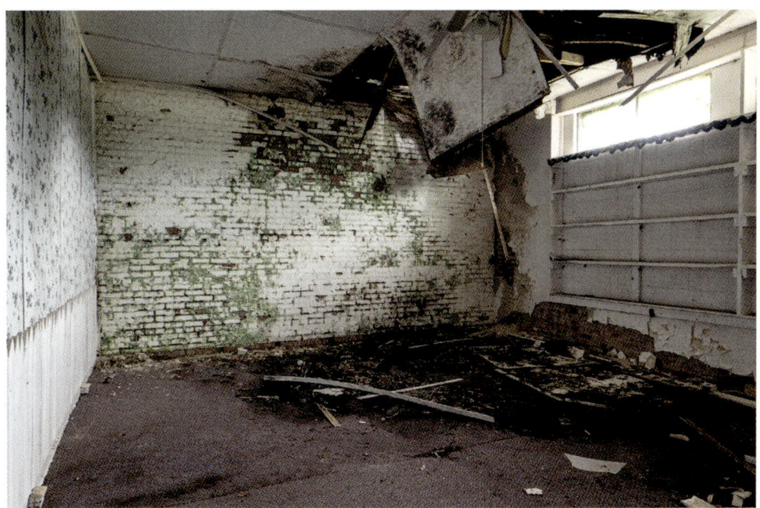

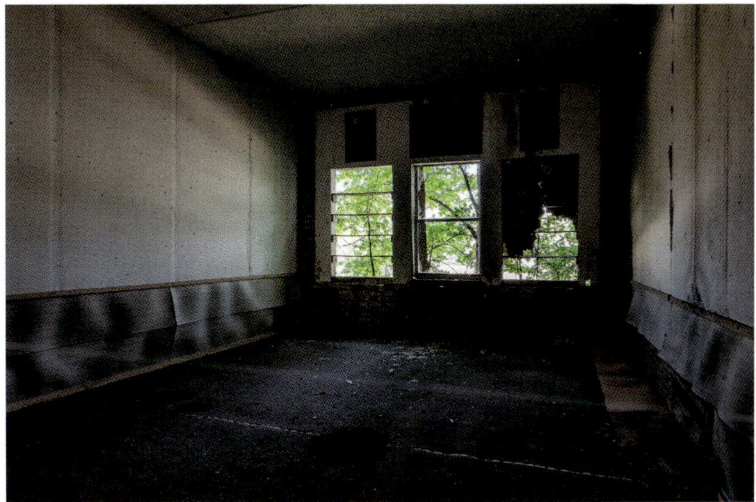

The main office.

## THE IVY ROOM

The last room on the west end of the building is the most interesting. Located next to the west entrance, this room served as a history and social sciences classroom. However, the room is distinct in appearance from the others. I effectively dubbed it the "Ivy Room." A small opening in the north wall provides an entrance for ivy, which sprawls across the walls and floors. The room fascinated me so much that I often returned to document how the ivy grew across the room during the spring and summer months.

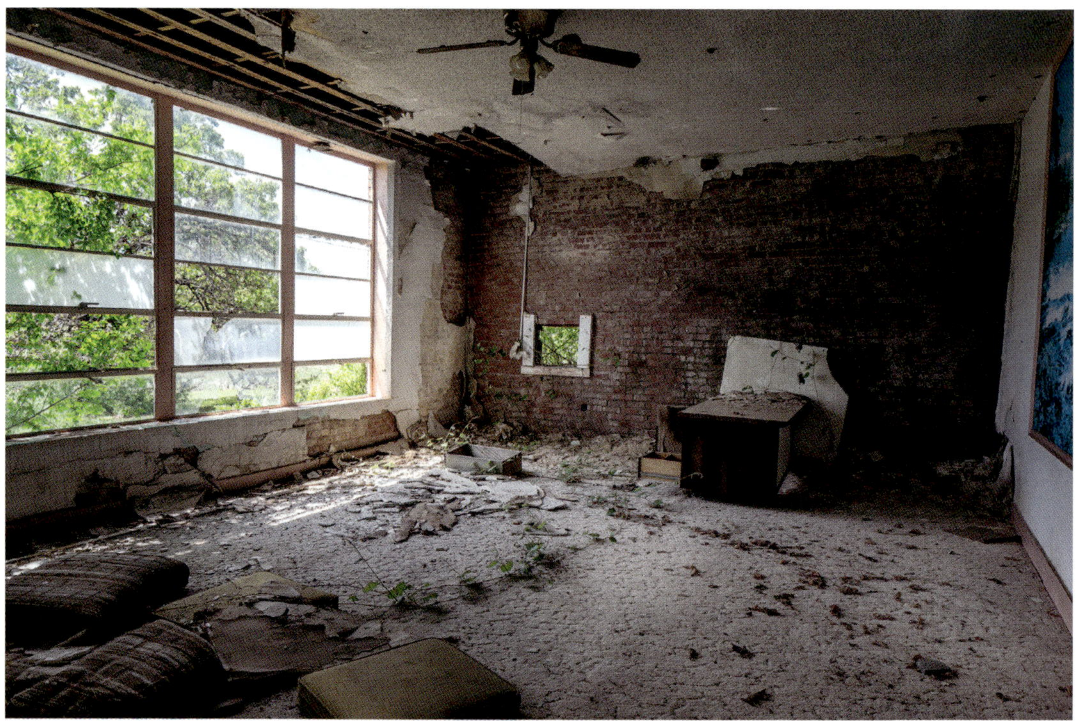

The Ivy Room. Former history and social sciences classroom. Various stages of ivy growth from spring to summer months.

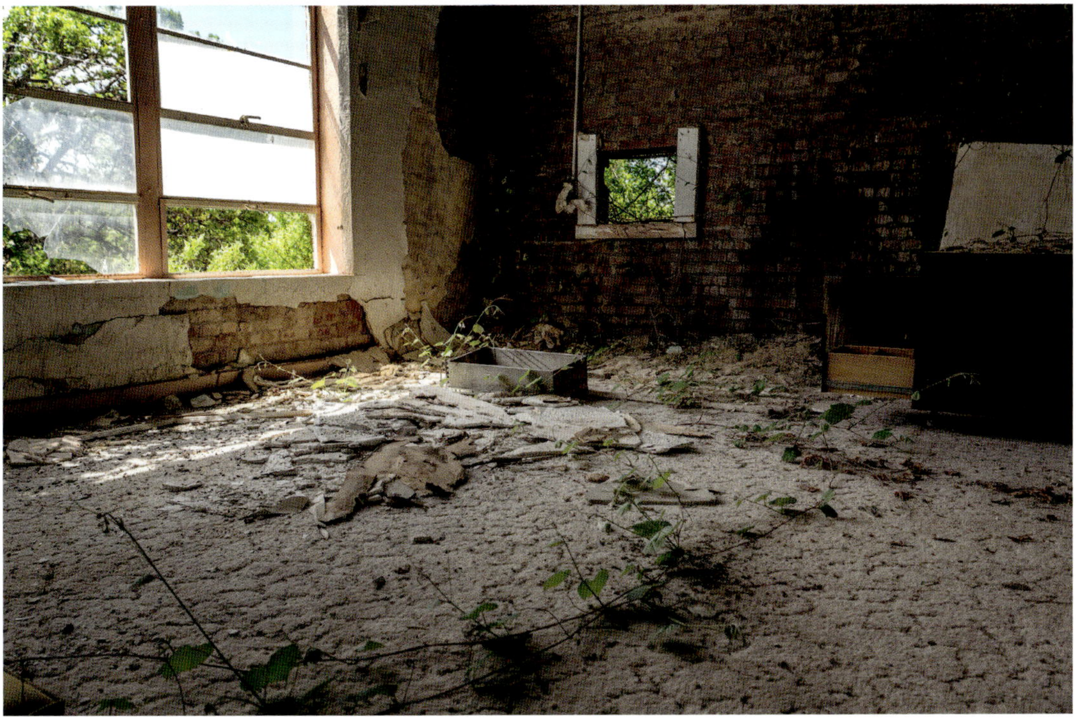

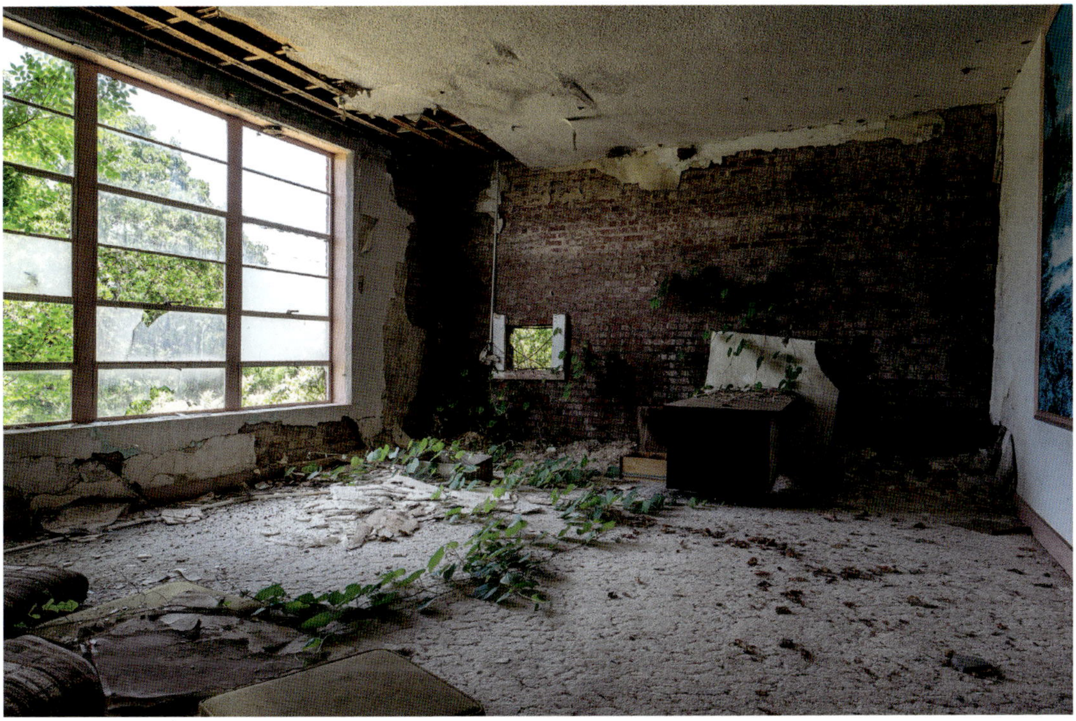

The Ivy Room in early spring.

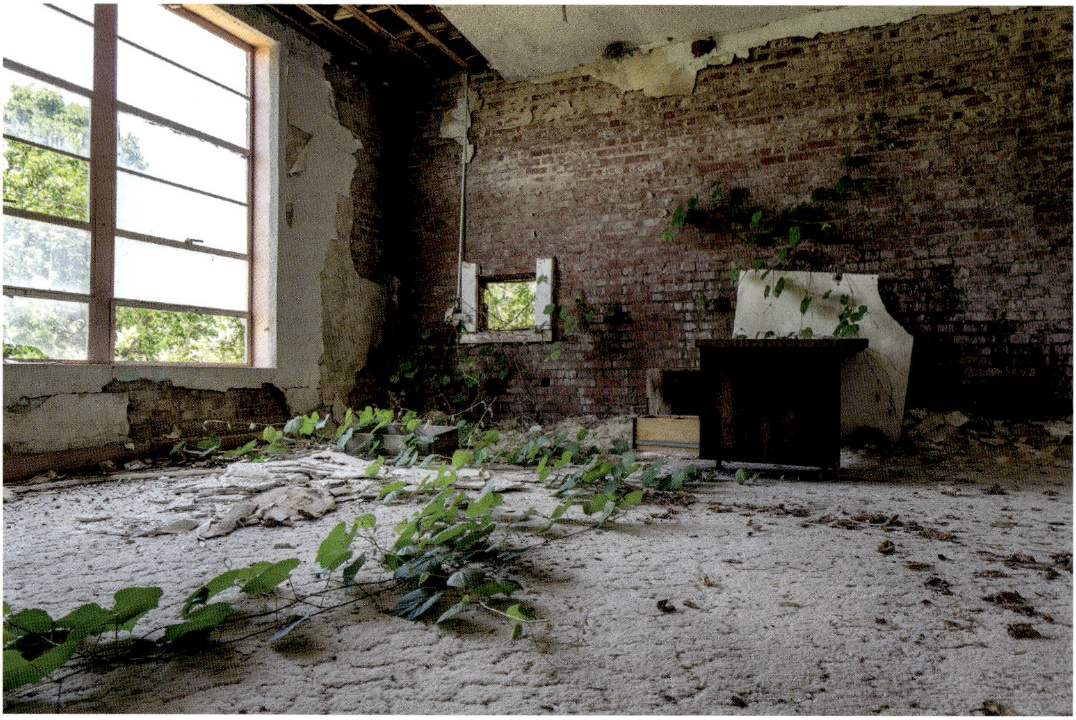

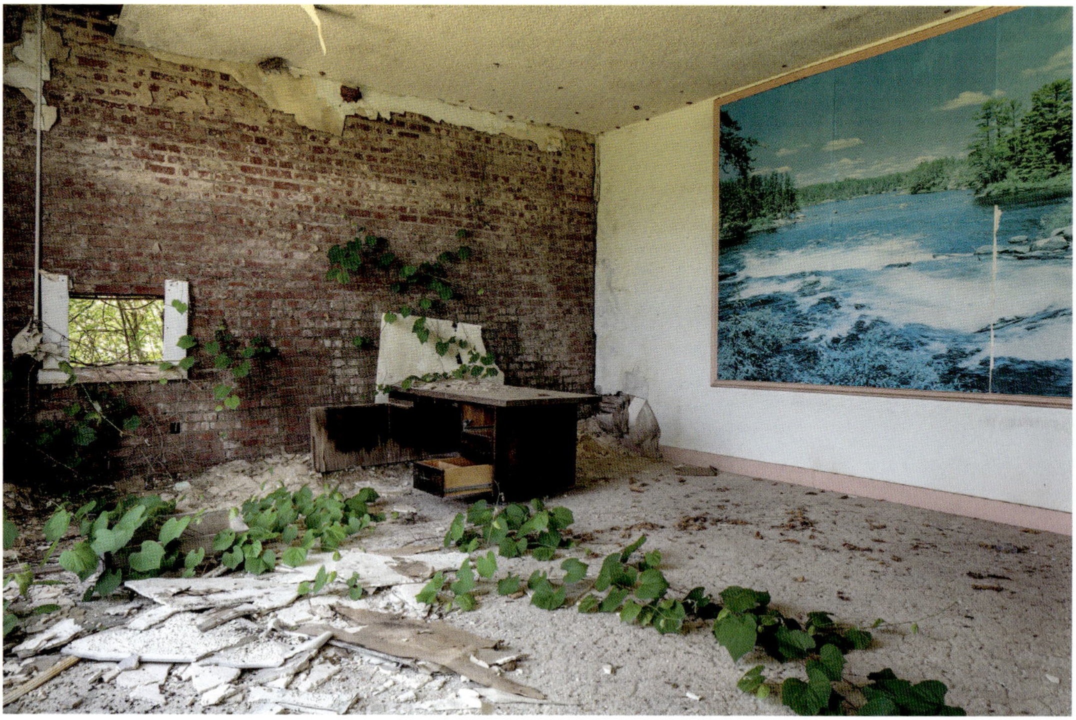

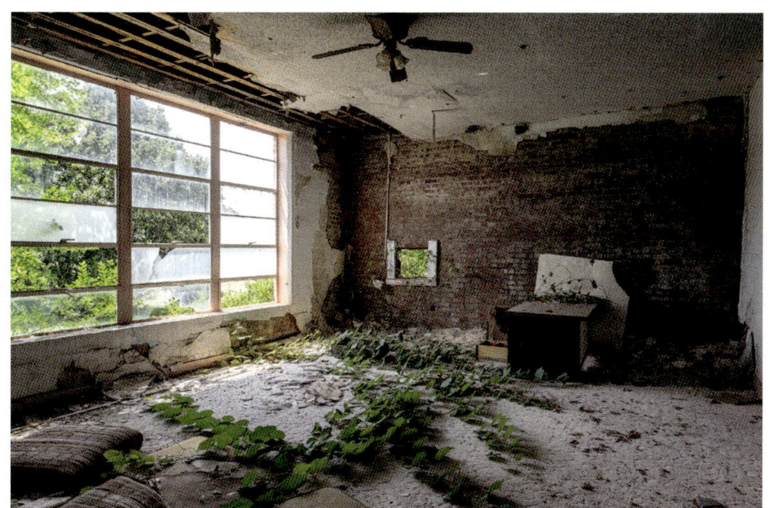

The Ivy Room in late spring.

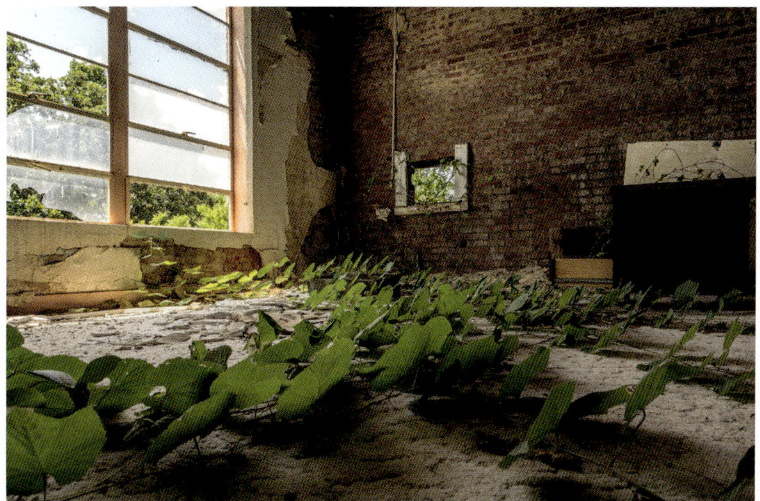

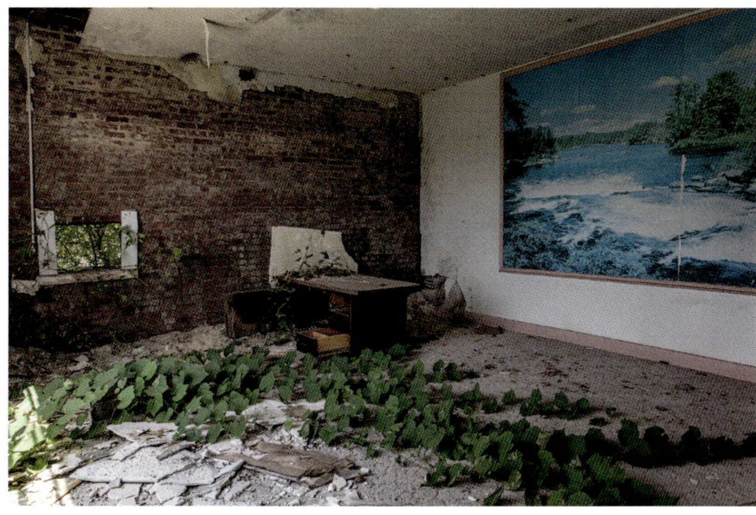

4

# A WALK AROUND THE GROUNDS

Little pictorial history exists that documents the layout of Harjo and surrounding structures. Even with first-hand accounts, visualizing original extremities is a challenge. The south lawn served additional purposes in addition to administrative and teacher housing. A playground existed here; however, all traces of it are long gone. A turnaround once provided a means for buses and parents to drop off students. A bus barn was also located on the property, but its exact location could not be verified.

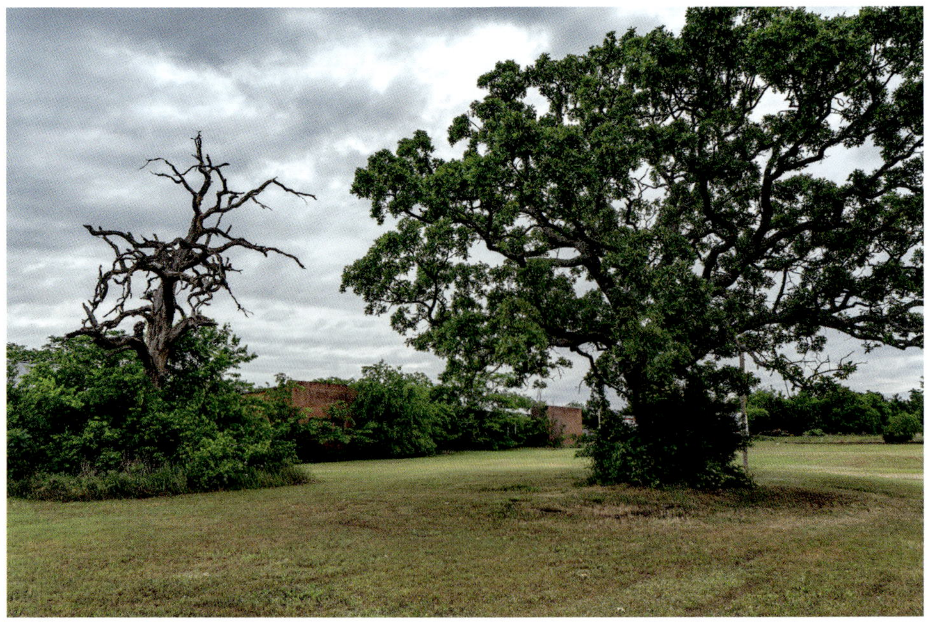

Trees on the south lawn. All signs of the former playground are now gone.

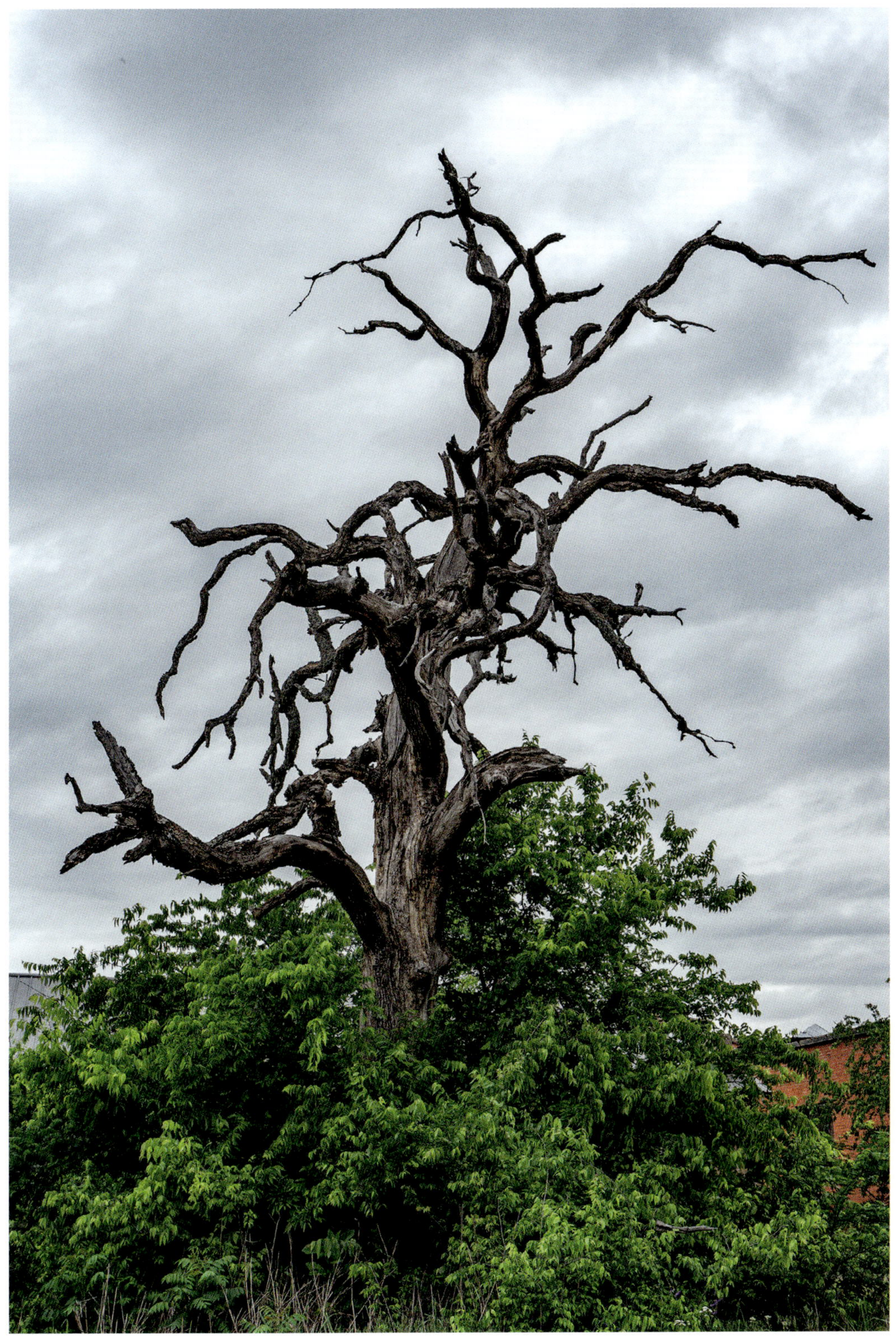

## The Cafeteria

A stone structure lies to the west of the main building. It was the same structure that first caught my attention and prompted me to investigate Harjo. The structure I had been drawn to was the school cafeteria. At one time, it was divided and also used for shop class. On the east end of the building are the school's bathrooms. The main facility did not have indoor plumbing, and students would have to go outside to access the cafeteria and use the facilities. The building is now occupied by a small business that rents the space.

While the building appears large outside, students have indicated that space was limited and the cafeteria was relatively small. The outside of the building is constructed from stone. There are no placards, but the building has the appearance of a Civilian Conservation Core or Works Progress Administration project (CCC and WPA). While the CCC and WPA were not created until the 1930s, there is no significant historical information to confirm when the cafeteria was constructed or if it would have been built as a result of one of these programs. Former students, however, state they remember seeing placards on both the school and cafeteria.

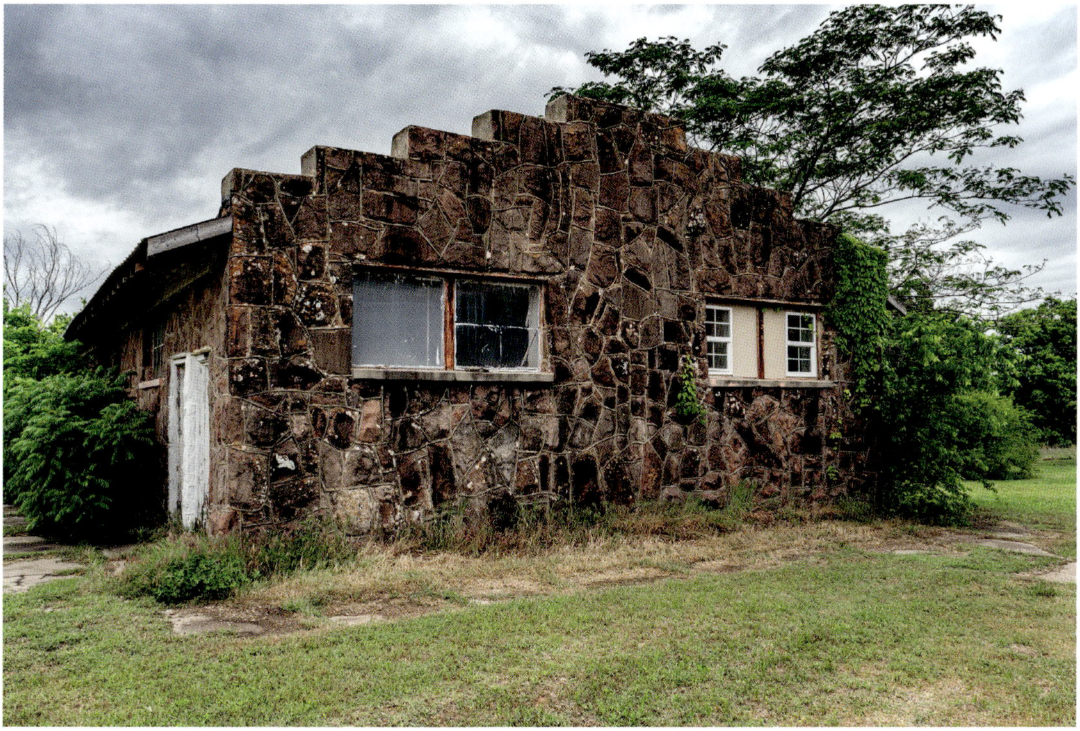

The old cafeteria resembles the work of CCC or WPA projects.

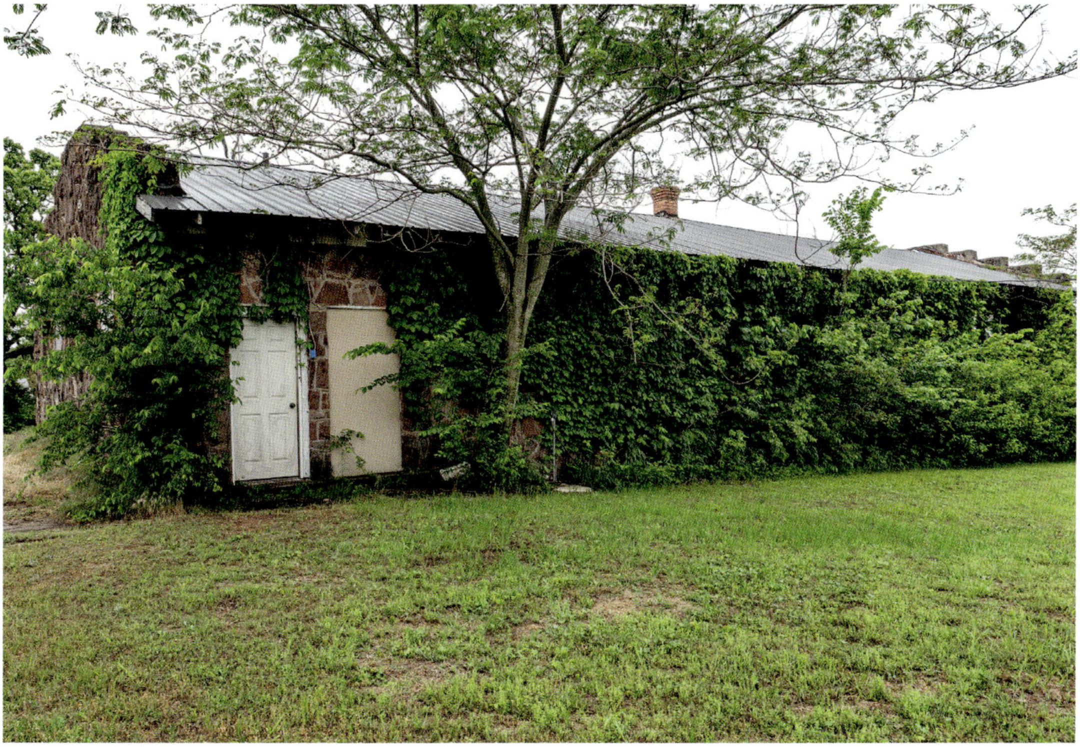

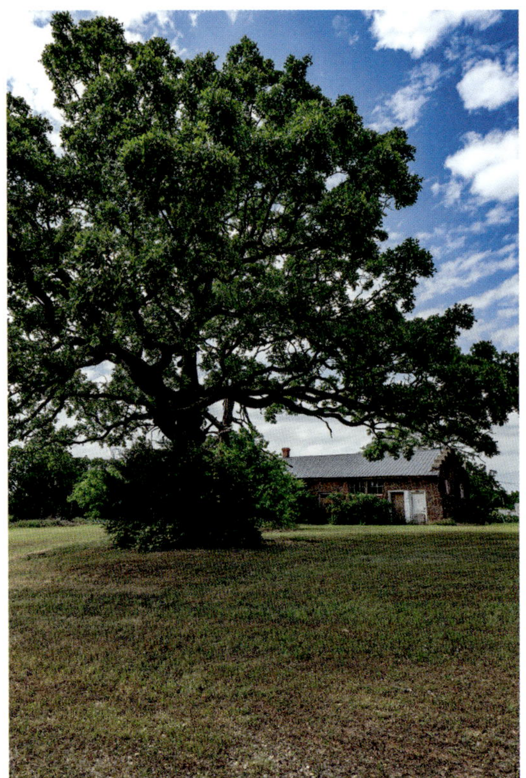

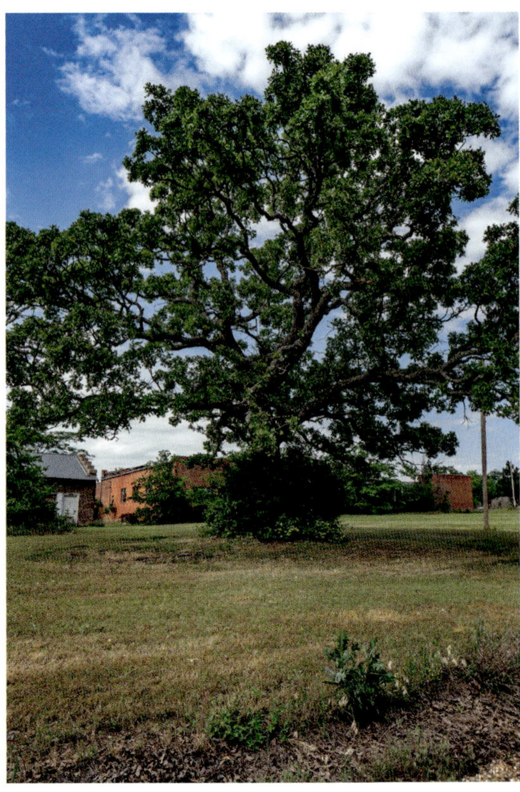

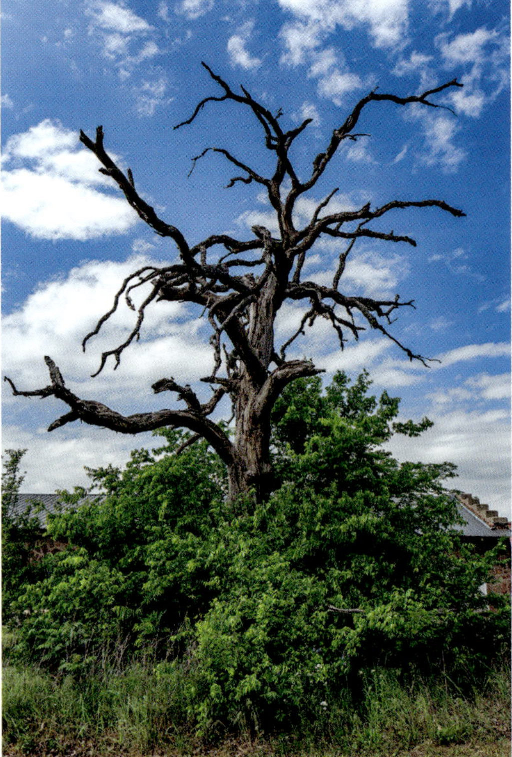

The old cafeteria can be seen just behind trees located on the south lawn near the playground area.

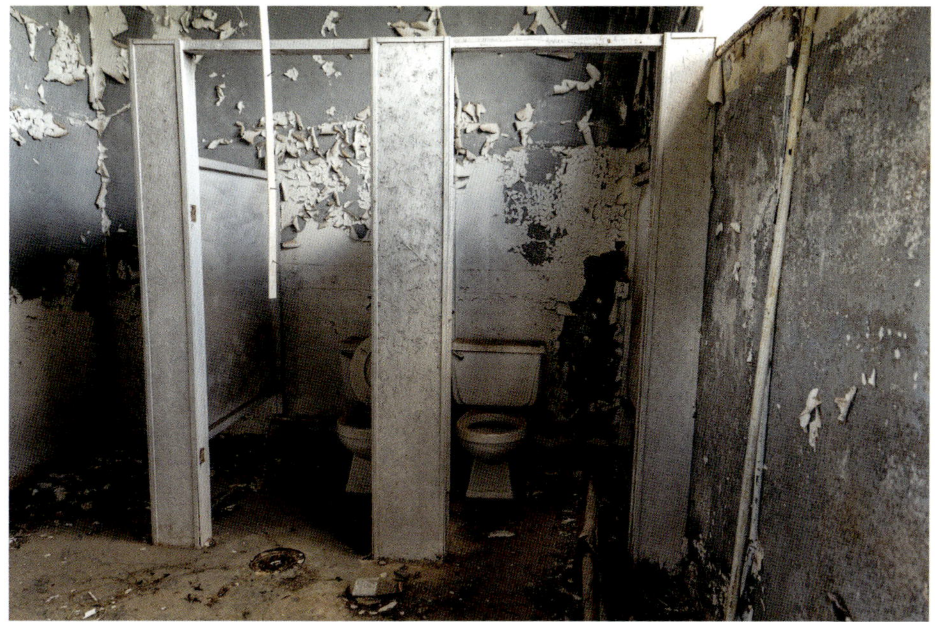

Students would need to go outside to access the bathrooms that were attached to the cafeteria.

## The CCC and WPA in Oklahoma

The Oklahoma landscape is strewn with CCC and WPA buildings. Most are placarded to designate the year of construction and which group was given credit. Often they are easy to identify, and many towns boast more of these buildings than others.

America was rising from the ashes of the Great Depression, and in 1933, Franklin Roosevelt created the Civilian Conservation Corps (CCC). The program was designed to create a new emergency response agency that could provide unskilled laborers with work. The CCC often employed individuals in rural communities. Enrollees could be tasked with any number of physically demanding projects, including building roadways, clearing forests, constructing dams, an array of construction projects, and emergency relief aid from natural disasters. Enrollees could serve anywhere between six and twenty-four months.[1]

Like the CCC, the Works Progress Administration (WPA) was also created under the Roosevelt Administration and it was established in 1935. WPA workers performed many of the same tasks as those who worked under the CCC; however, the primary difference was that WPA workers were certified by the administration. Both men and women could work under the WPA, but only one member per household was allowed to enroll.[2]

Applicants from age eighteen could apply for work with no upper age limit. People with disabilities were also welcome to apply. The National Youth Administration was a WPA branch that employed students between sixteen and twenty-four years old. After eighteen months, workers were terminated from employment to ensure that work could be granted to as many people as possible.[3]

## The Gym

Outside and to the north of the school are the ruins of a once-prominent gym. The facility is no stranger to disaster, and it has been destroyed on two separate occasions. The first was in approximately 1965 when a tornado obliterated the original facility. An exact replica was later rebuilt. However, in 2007 the gym fell victim to arson.

Dances, roller skating, and of course, basketball games are among some of the memories shared by the current owner. Former students shared similar sentiments. The owner shared some of her cherished memories are of the facility:

> I loved the gym. It had this amazing honeycomb sort of ceiling and a very specific smell. It seemed so enormous to me. I remember climbing all over the bleachers and the score box. One of my earliest memories was skating there and being swung around by older cousins. In the eighties, the couple that owned it [...] would have church meetings that we would go to as well as community outreach. My family had a wedding, a reunion, and a thanksgiving there sometime too.

All that remains are the ashen ruins of the mostly hollowed-out gym. It is hard to imagine what it would have looked like as there is little left to the imagination. Save for a few wood support beams and crumbling walls, the building is unrecognizable as a gym.

A ticket counter and concession window greeted patrons at the front entrance that is now laden with rubble. Cinderblock is strewn about like a minefield. The footing is much more treacherous than it first appears, and one must watch their step. Boys and girls locker rooms were located at the south and north ends of the building, respectively. A supply closet, coach's office, and utility room were located on the northeast corner.

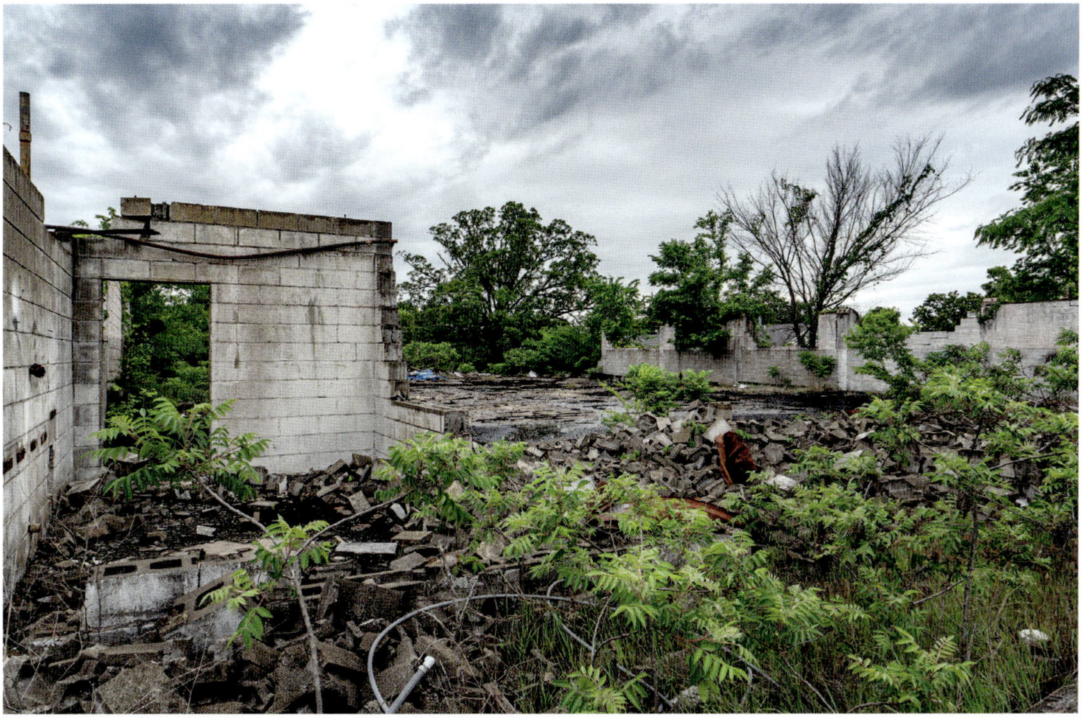

Entrance to the old gym, now in ruin.

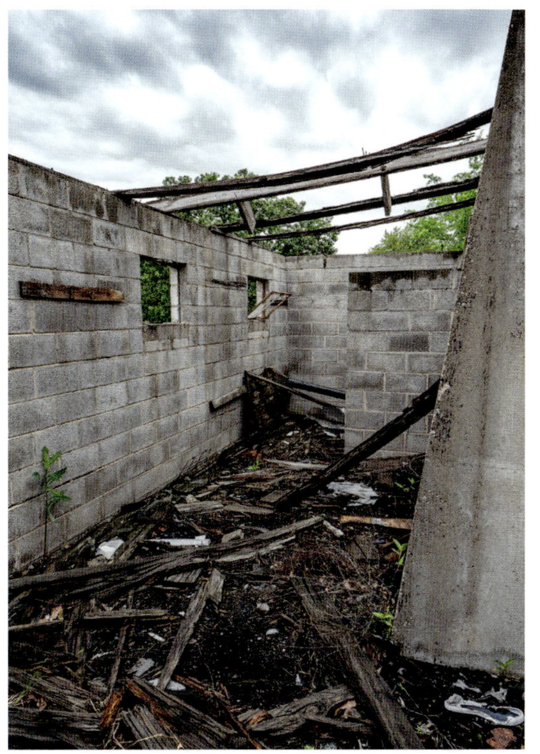

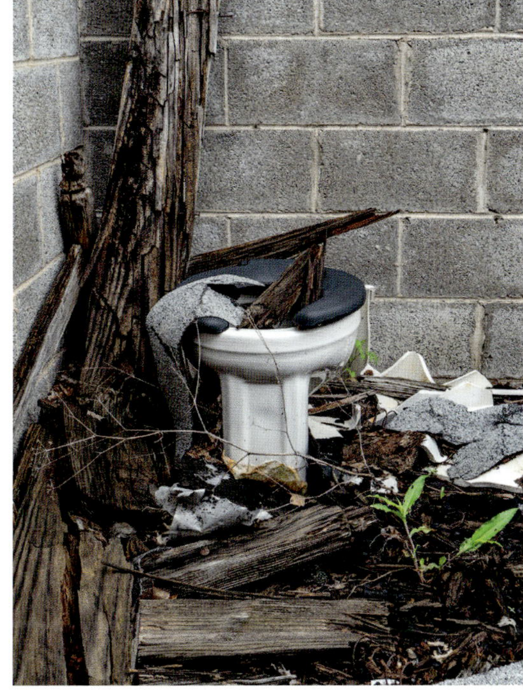

The boy's gym locker room.

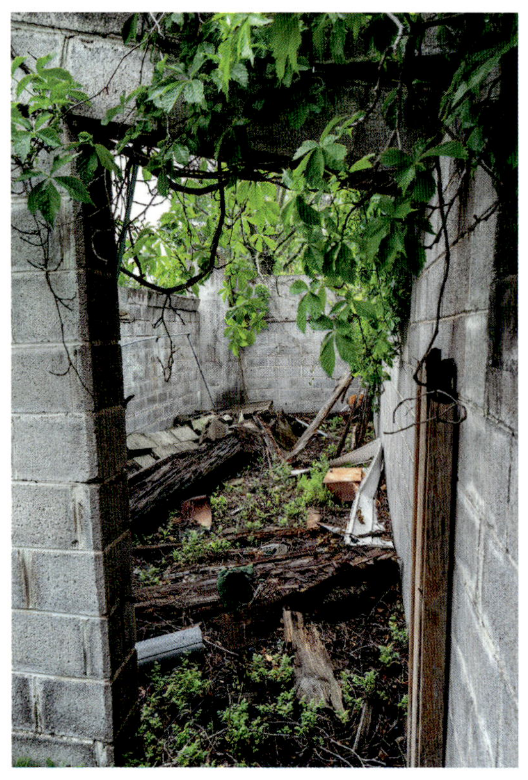

Entrance to girl's gym locker room.

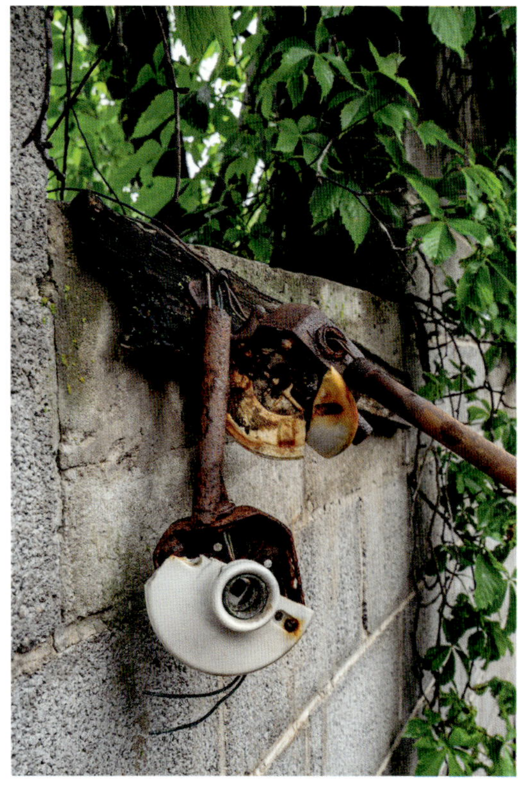

A collapsed light fixture inside the old storage room.

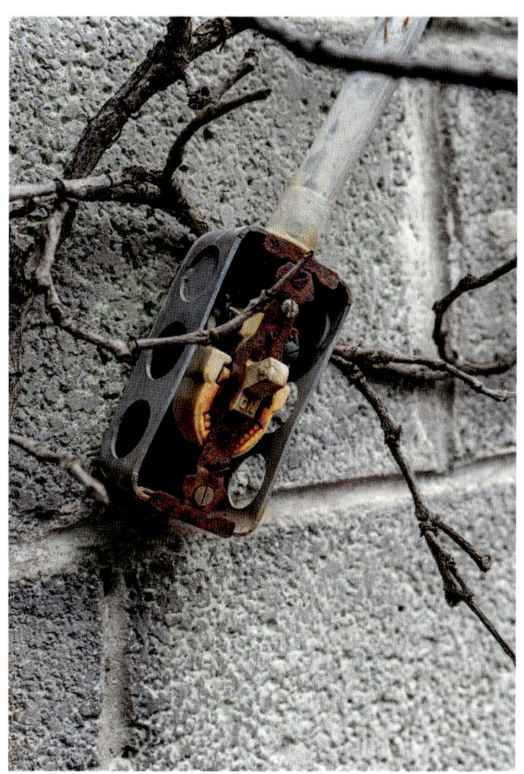

A light switch hangs in the hallway between the coach's office and storage room.

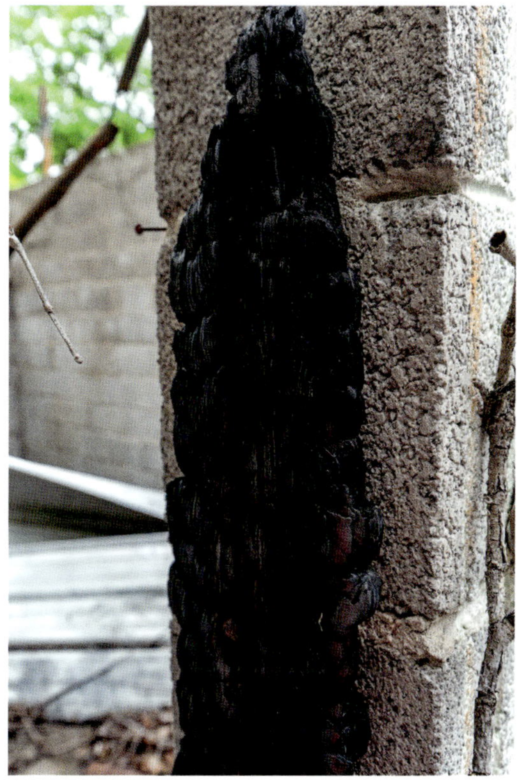

The charred doorway to the coach's office.

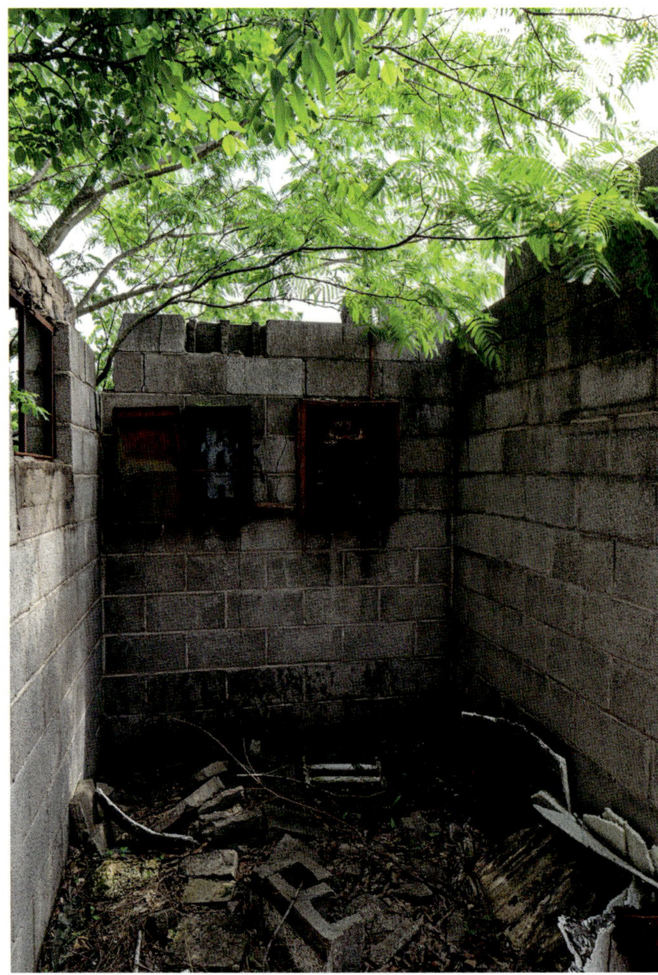

An old utility closet with breaker boxes still mounted on the wall.

The concrete foundation would have been covered with wood planking. Now the burned support system that anchored the panels to the concrete is all that is left. Metal anchors precariously protrude from the concrete and ensure that tetanus vaccine manufacturers will be in business for decades to come. The anchors are firmly in place and penetrate footwear with ease. Avoiding them is almost impossible.

Glass, molten metal, wires, and burned wood litter every square inch of the gym. Wood beams and ceiling anchors are scattered like a shipwreck across the seafloor. Nature has crept back in and grows in almost every crevice possible, from moss to vines.

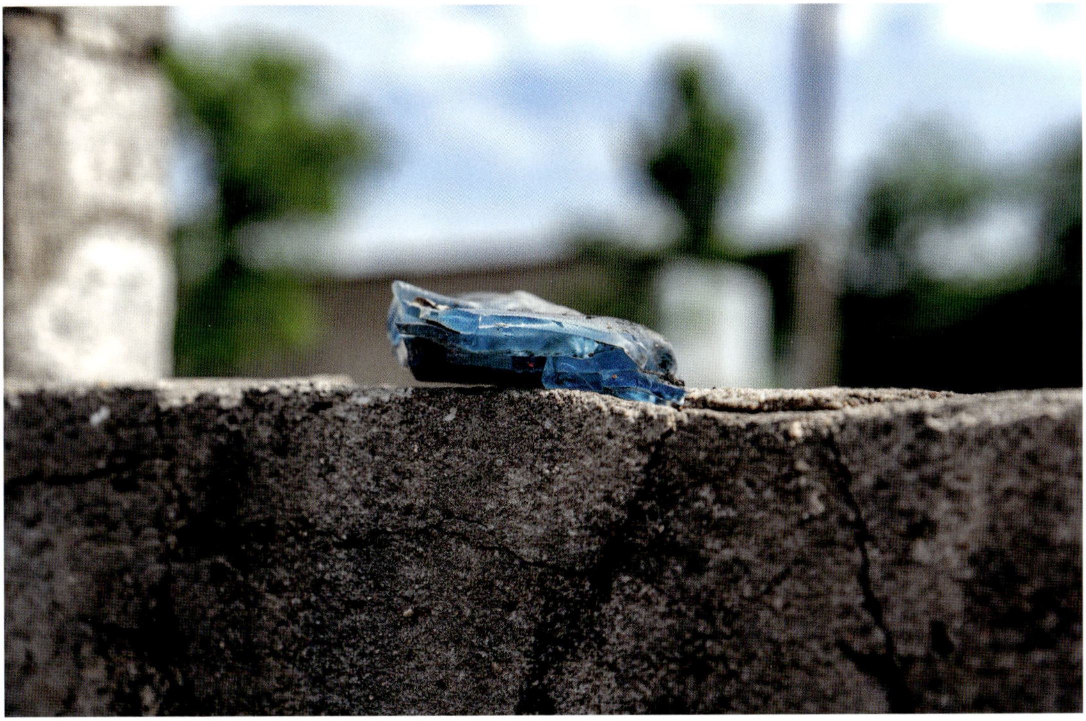

Pieces of molten glass rest atop of an outer wall.

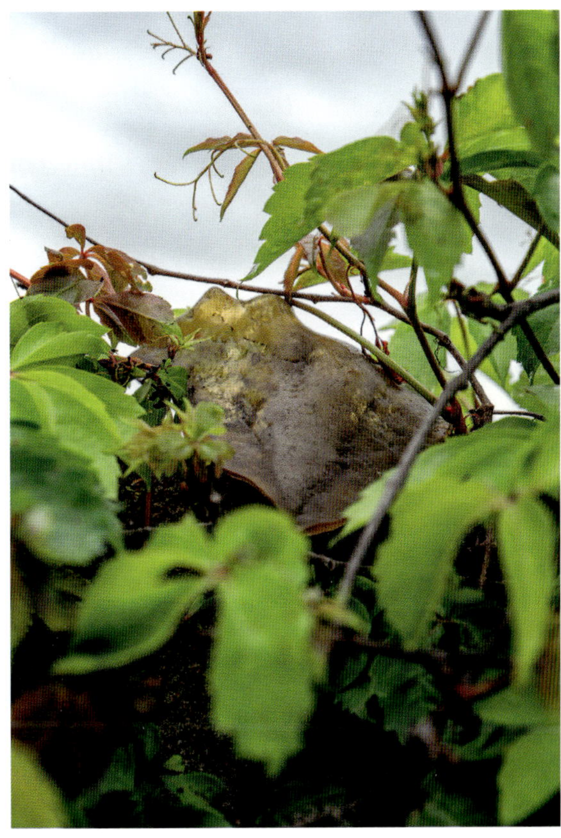

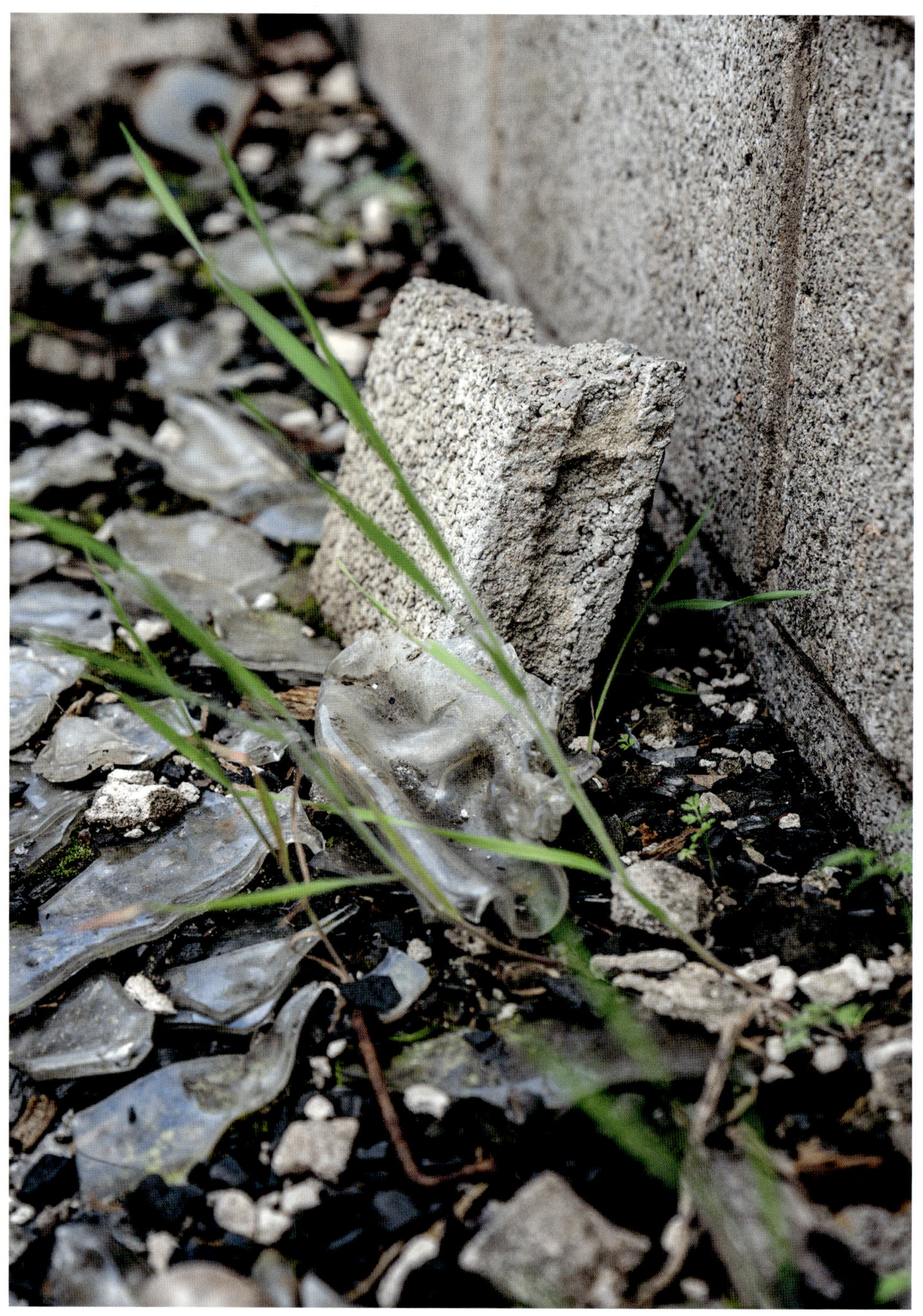

Shards of molten glass, charred wood fragments, and debris are scattered about.

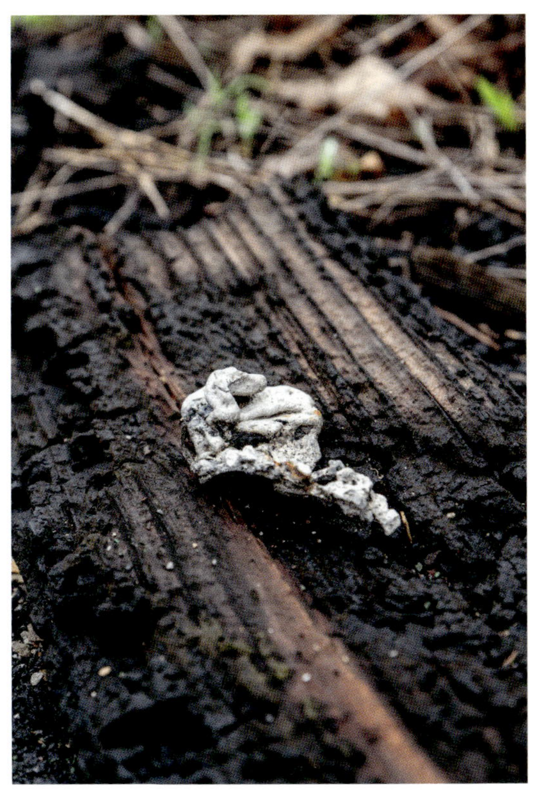

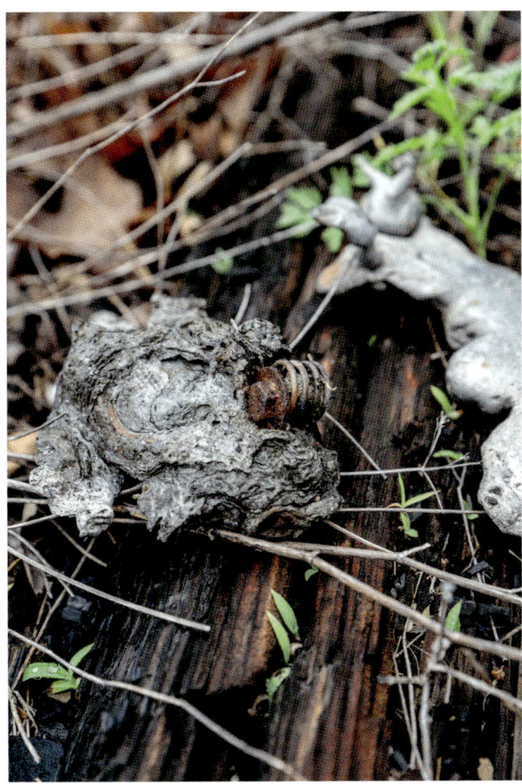

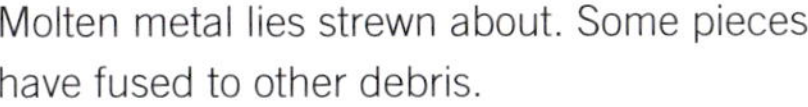

Molten metal lies strewn about. Some pieces have fused to other debris.

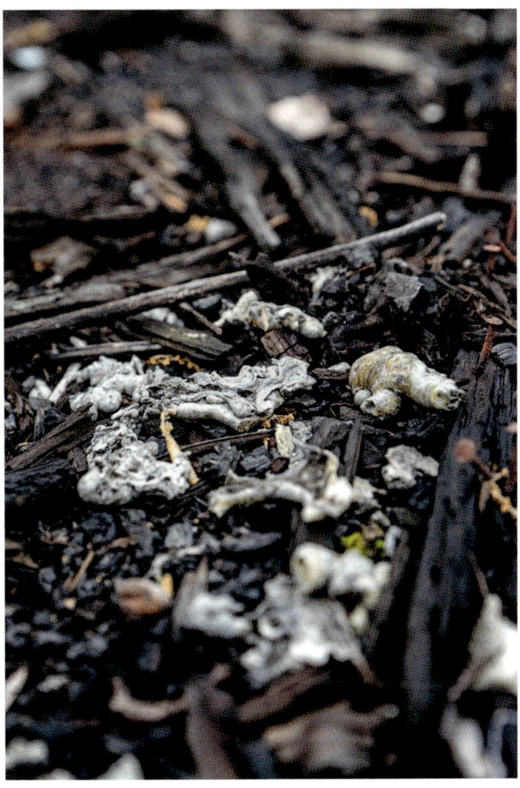

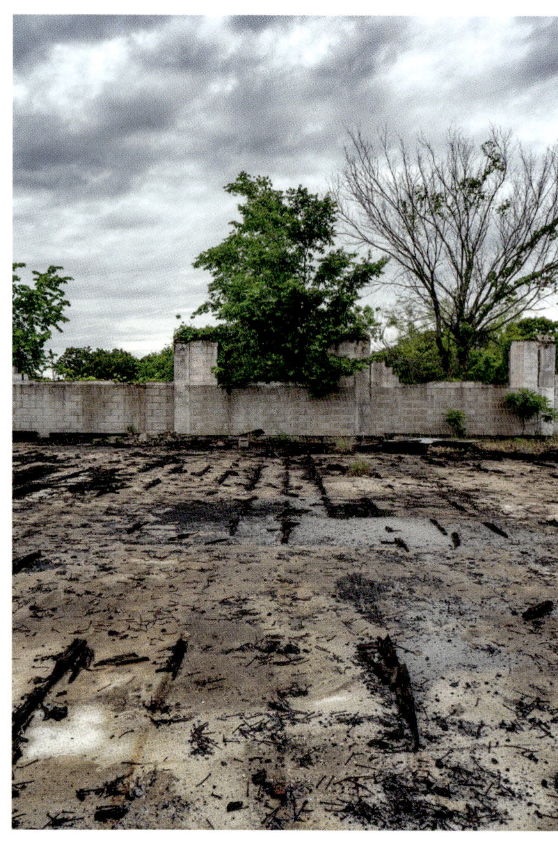

The gym's northern wall and concrete foundation. Charred wood is still anchored to the floor.

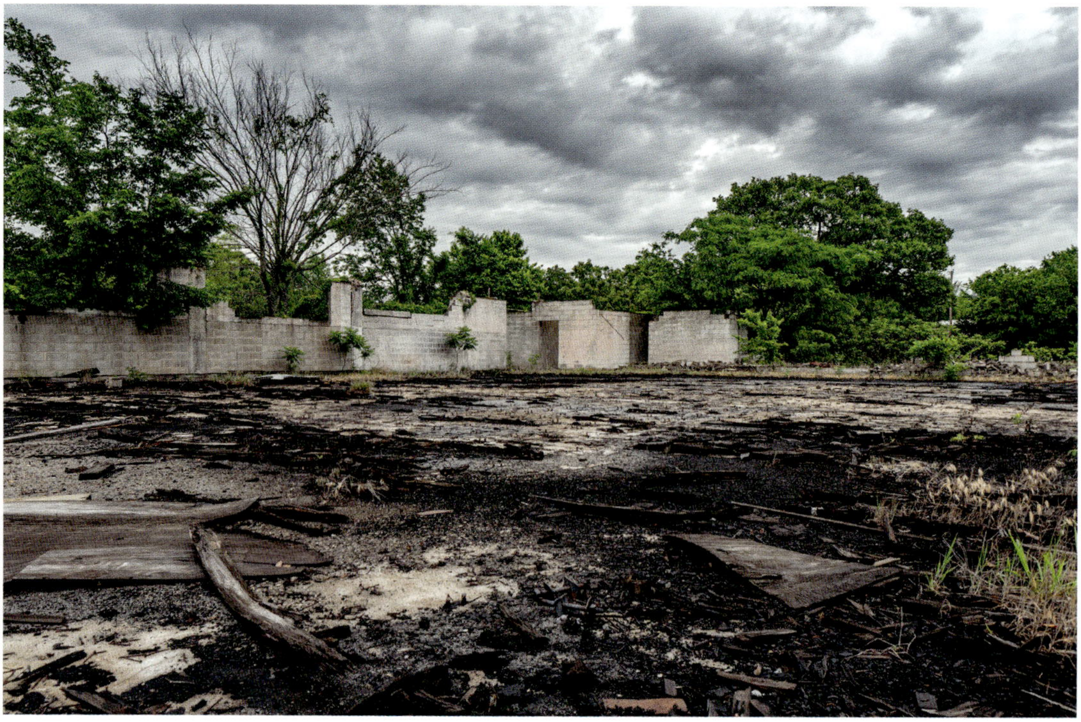

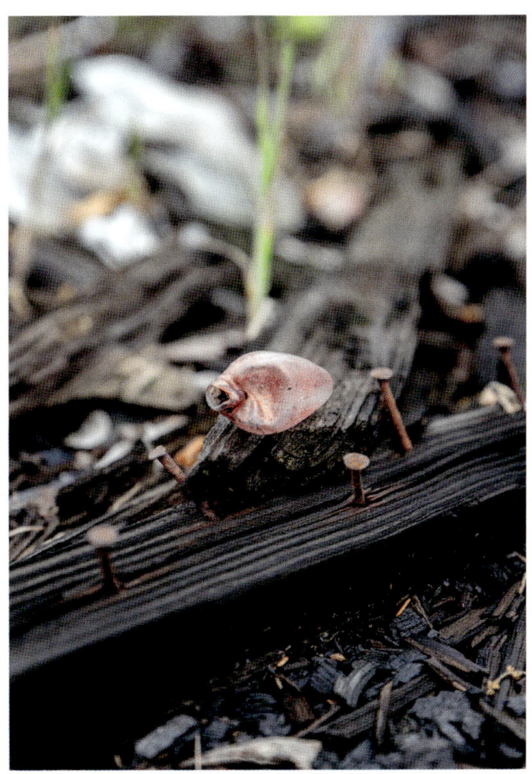

Molten glass, metal, party lights, a small motor, charred wood, and random debris scattered across the gym floor.

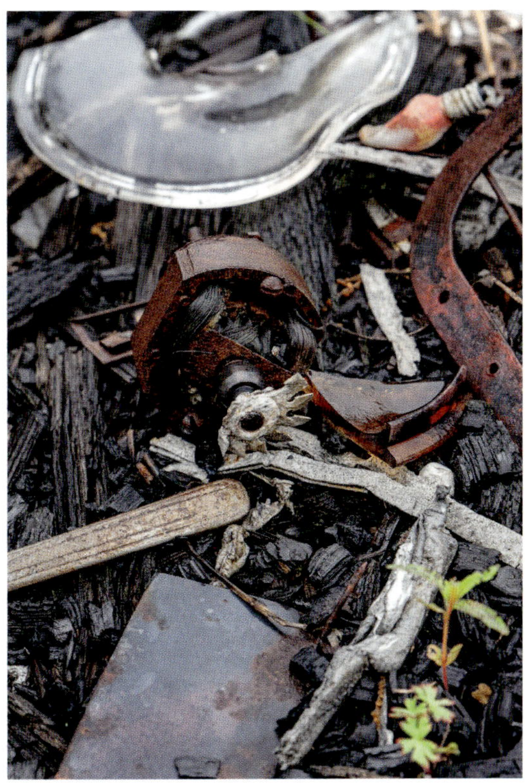

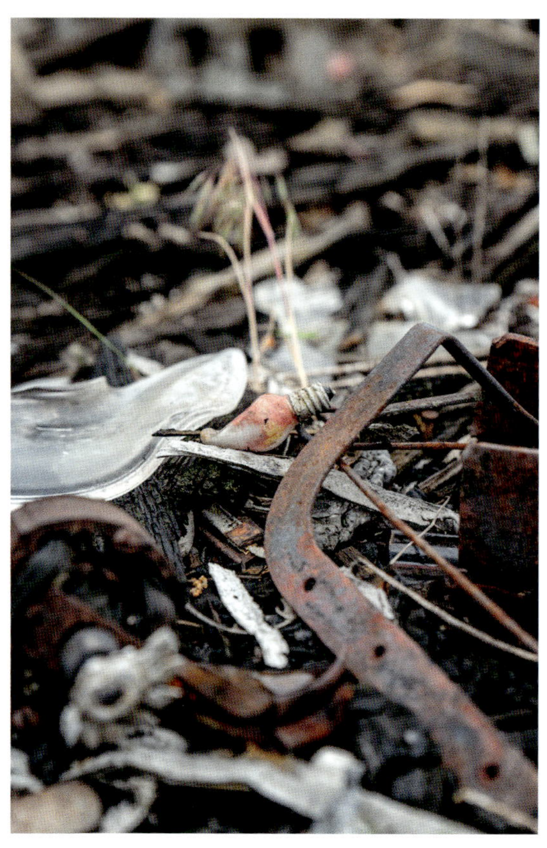

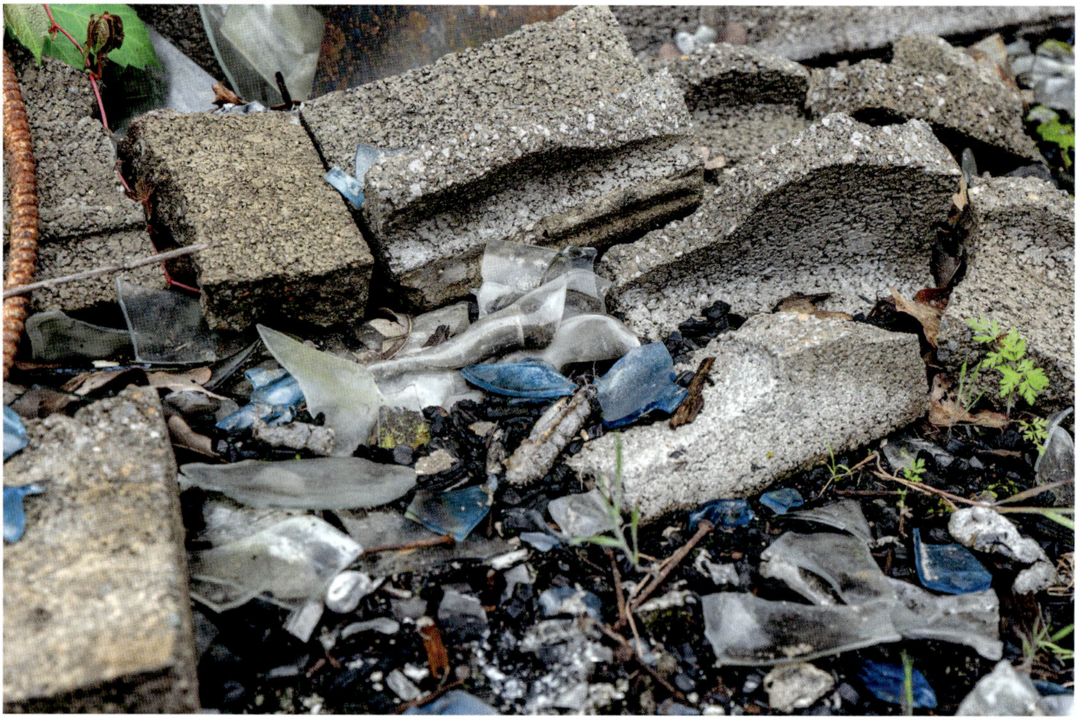

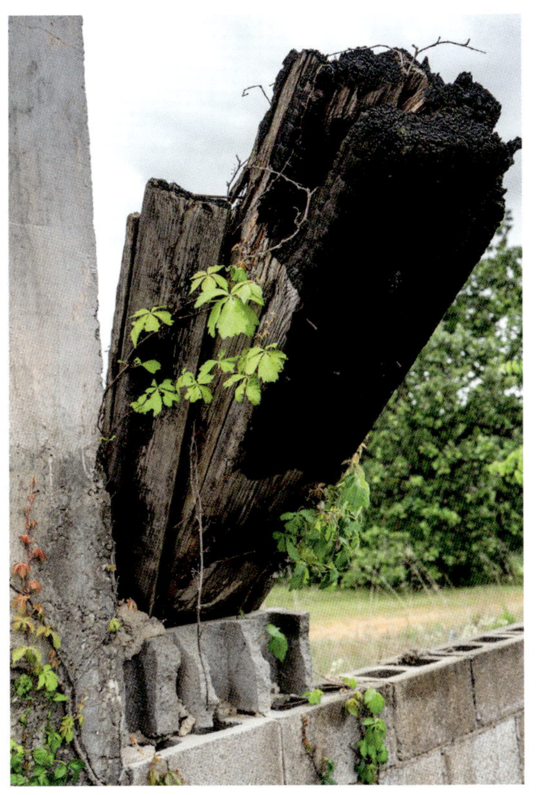

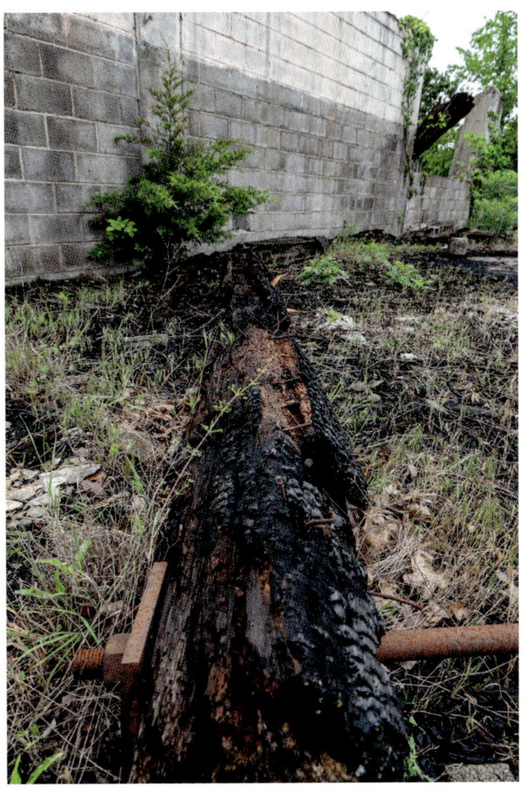

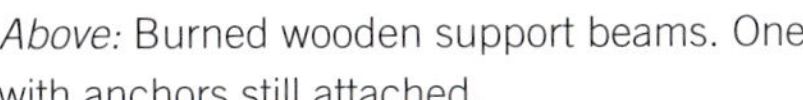

*Above:* Burned wooden support beams. One with anchors still attached.

*Right:* A support anchor lies nearby.

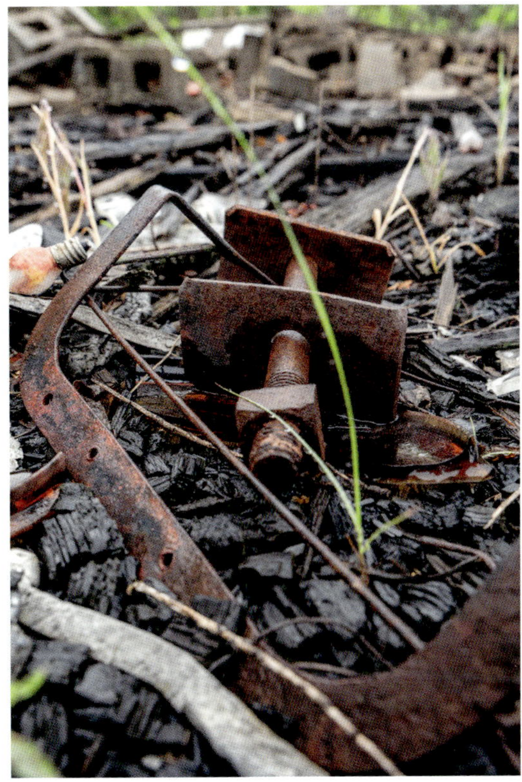

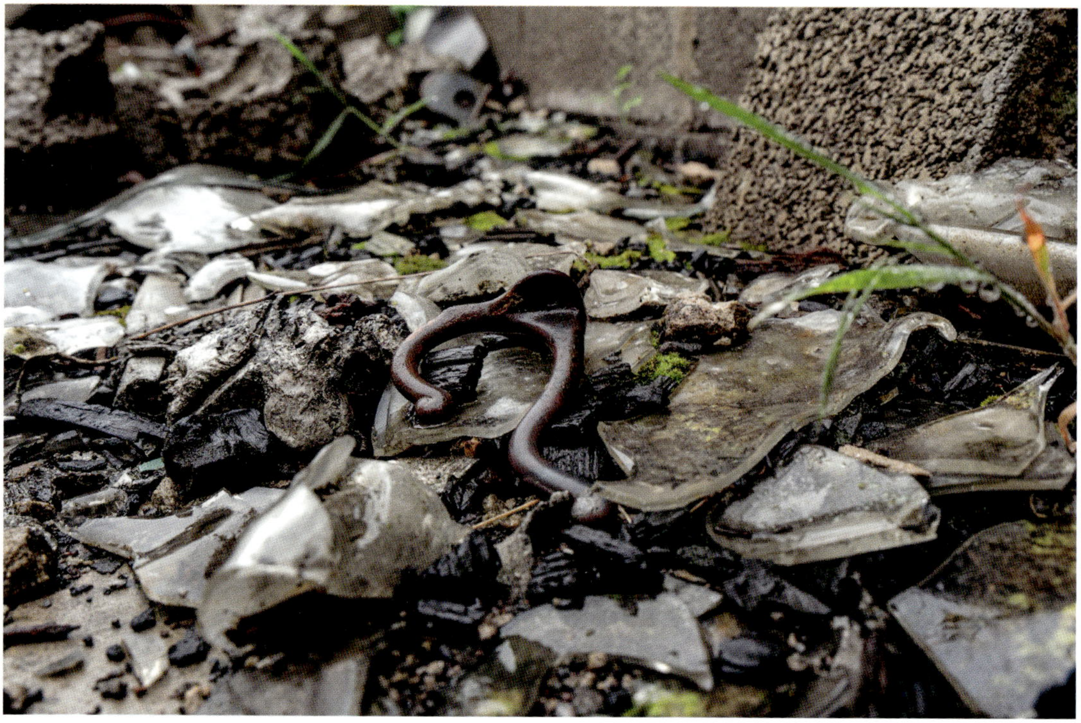

Debris, molten metal, and glass line the floors of the old gym.

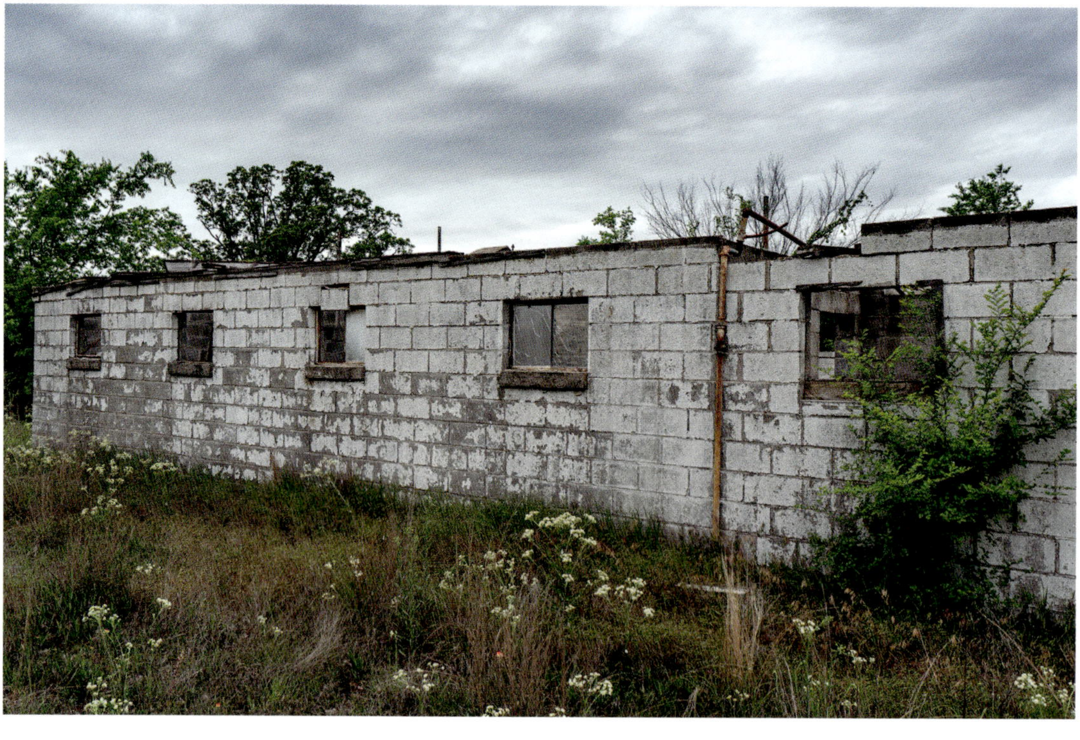

The south gym wall outside the boy's locker room.

## The Shower House and Cellar

A cinderblock shower house was constructed on the northeast corner of the school. However, no information exists regarding its history. Former alumni have indicated that it was most likely built after the school closed. One side of the structure is missing, but the other side is still intact. A water tank was placed to the east of the building for showers, sinks, and toilets. Older photos indicate that the structure was primarily used as storage after the school closed.

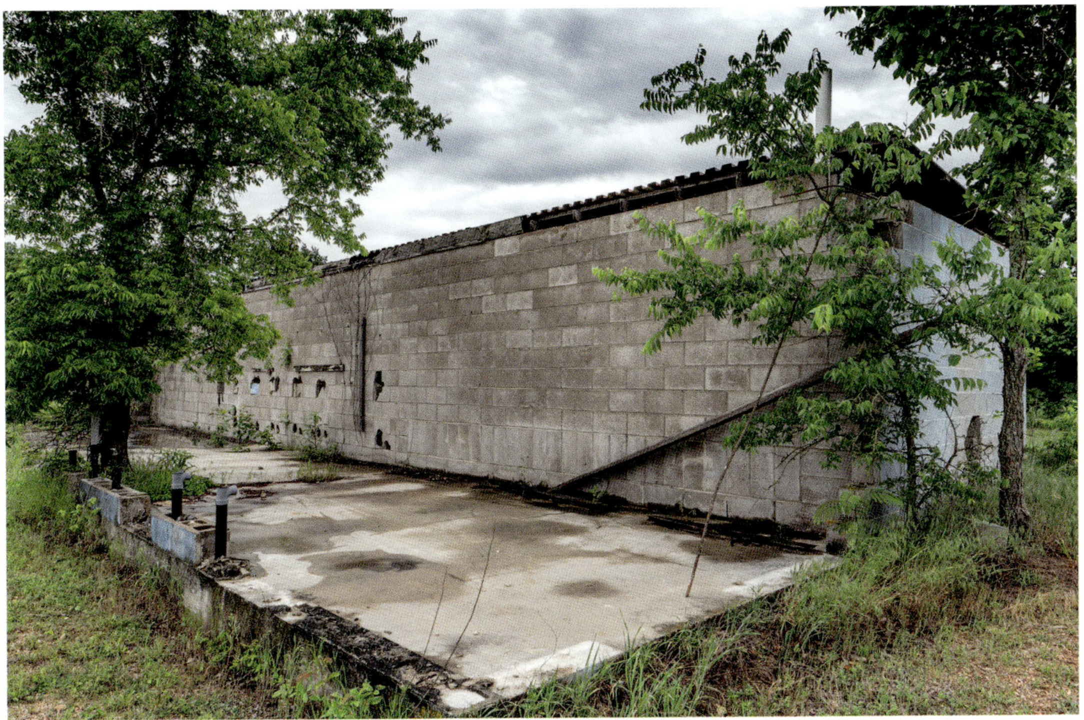

The exterior to the shower house and what would have been the north side of the enclosure.

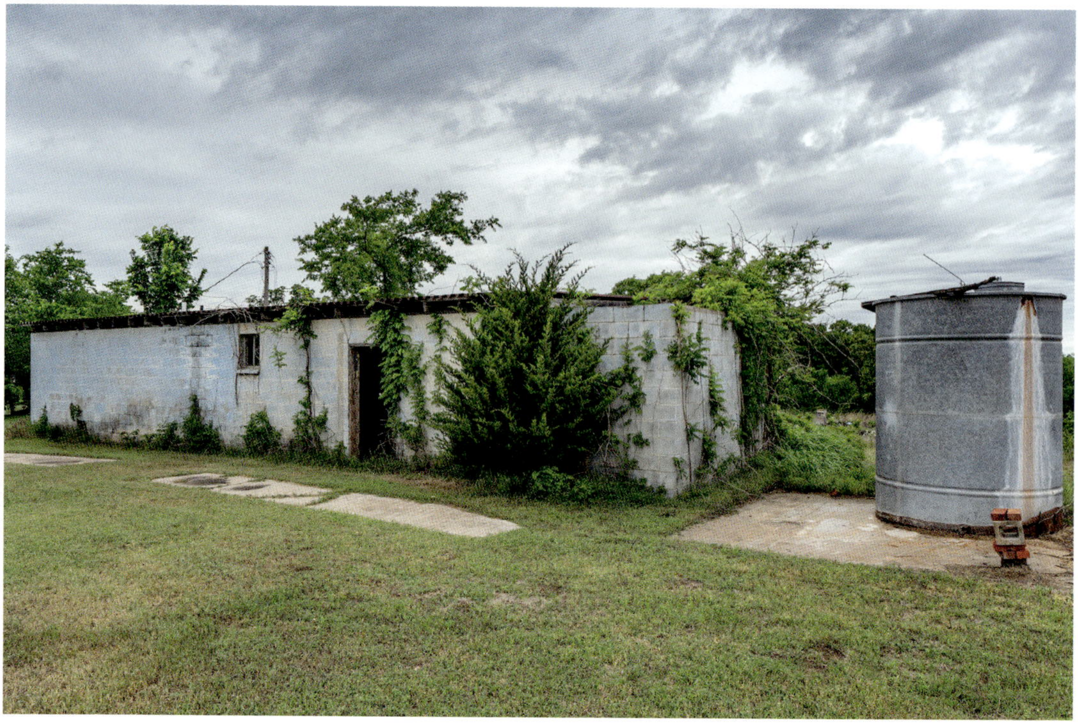

The south-facing exterior wall and entrance to the shower house. A water storage tank sits on the east side.

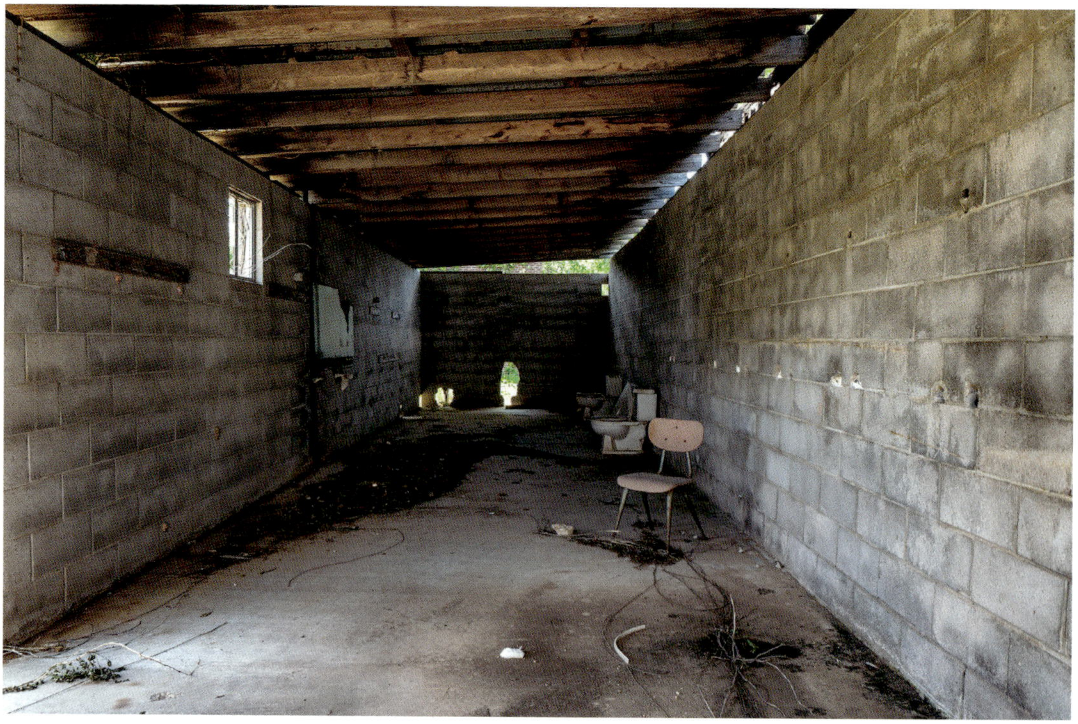

The interior enclosure of the southern portion of the shower house. Plumbing still protrudes from the walls and floors.

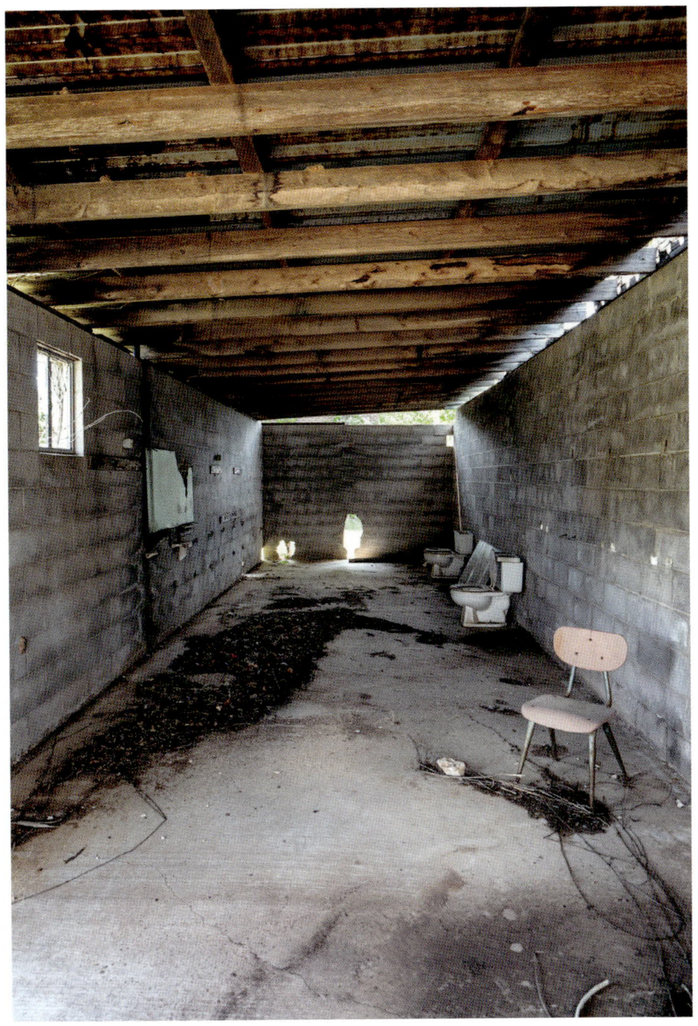

A cellar sits in front of the school and on the southeast corner. It was one of the largest I have ever seen, and a necessity in Oklahoma. Spring and summer weather can be unpredictable, and one never knows when there will be a need for immediate shelter. The cellar is dark, and the only source of light is from one of two entrances. As with many in-ground shelters, time takes its toll, and their ability to keep out the elements fades. This one currently holds approximately two inches of water, and being sealed up most of the year, chances of evaporation are next to slim. It is hard to imagine 300 students and faculty could fit in this area, but it is possible. The cellar is still in use today by local residents should the need arise.

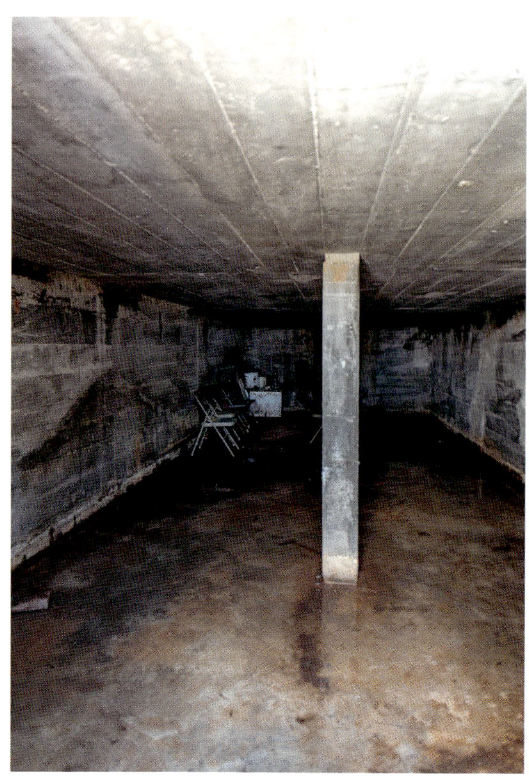

Standing water covers the entire floor of the cellar. A few chairs line the walls for residents to wait out a passing storm.

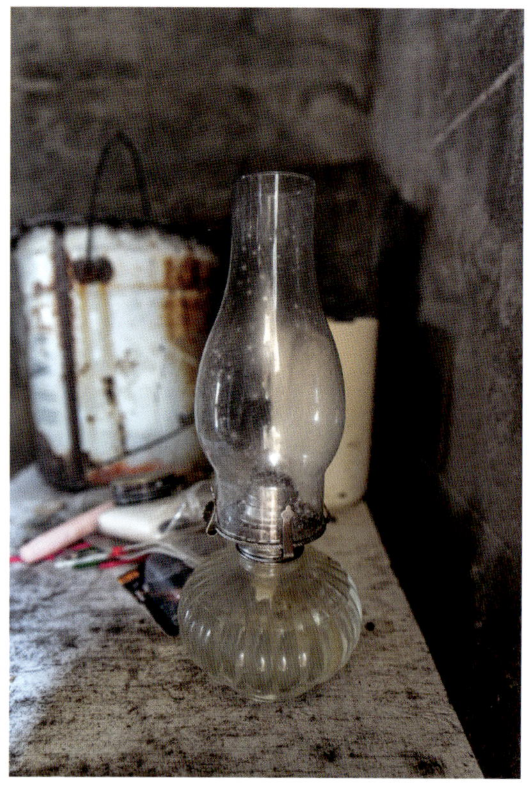

Personal effects litter a table, including a kerosene lamp.

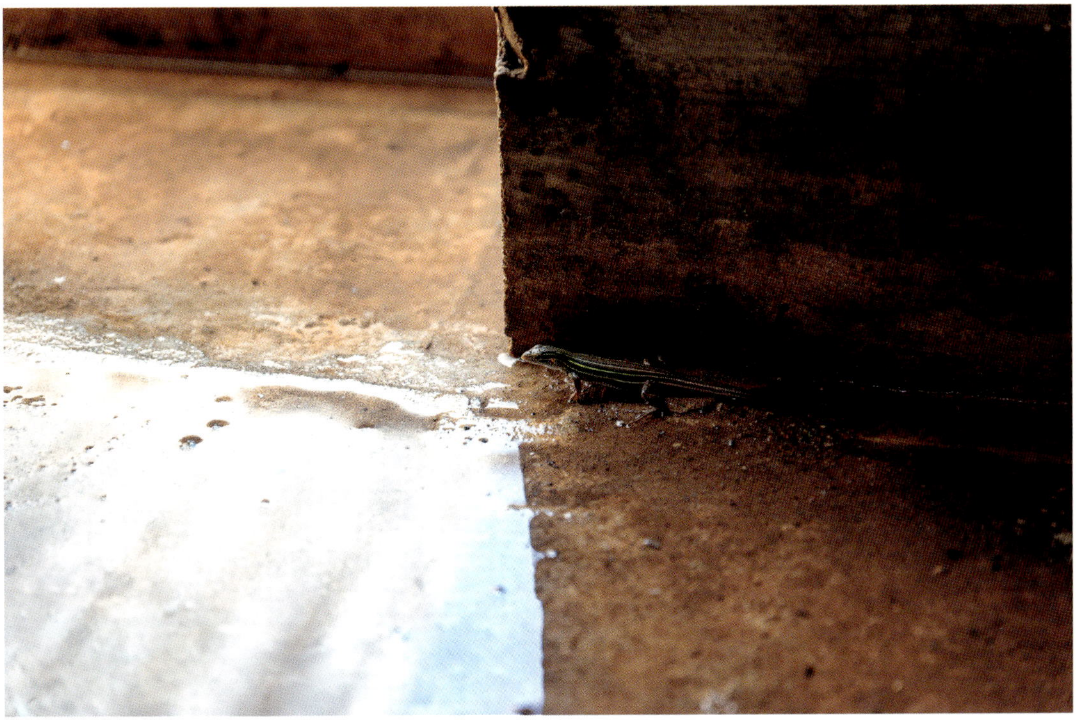

On this particular day, a salamander joined me and frolicked in the stagnant waters.

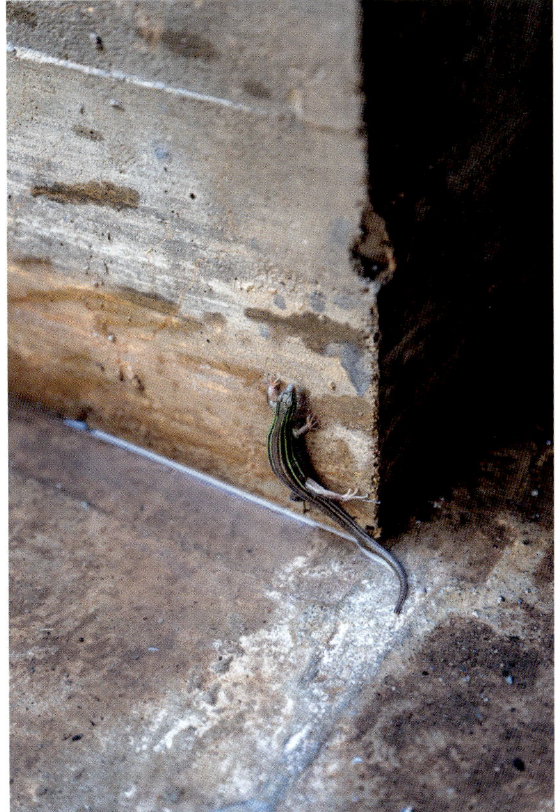

# 5

# HARJO FROM ABOVE

Harjo is decaying badly, and it is hard to discern how much longer it will stand. While the exterior walls and flooring appear to be sound, there is substantial damage to almost every room. Remodeling may be problematic, if not impossible. There is extensive roof damage. Aerial photos also show how much wear and decay has taken place. Heavy rains and Oklahoma winds have not been kind over the years.

The extent of damage to the old auditorium is far more apparent. Sheet metal has torn back with each gust of wind, exposing the bowels of the institution a fraction of an inch at a time. Each increase in exposure results in more places for rain, snow, and sunlight to inflict damage. All of this ripens the school's interior for mold and other life to grow even in the darkest corners.

Aerial images of the building indicate that the ceiling over the auditorium would have been taller at one time. At least one gable can be observed at the auditorium's north end. Former student testimony indicates that the roof was replaced due to tornado damage, and it may have been lowered around the same time as the construction of the new gym.

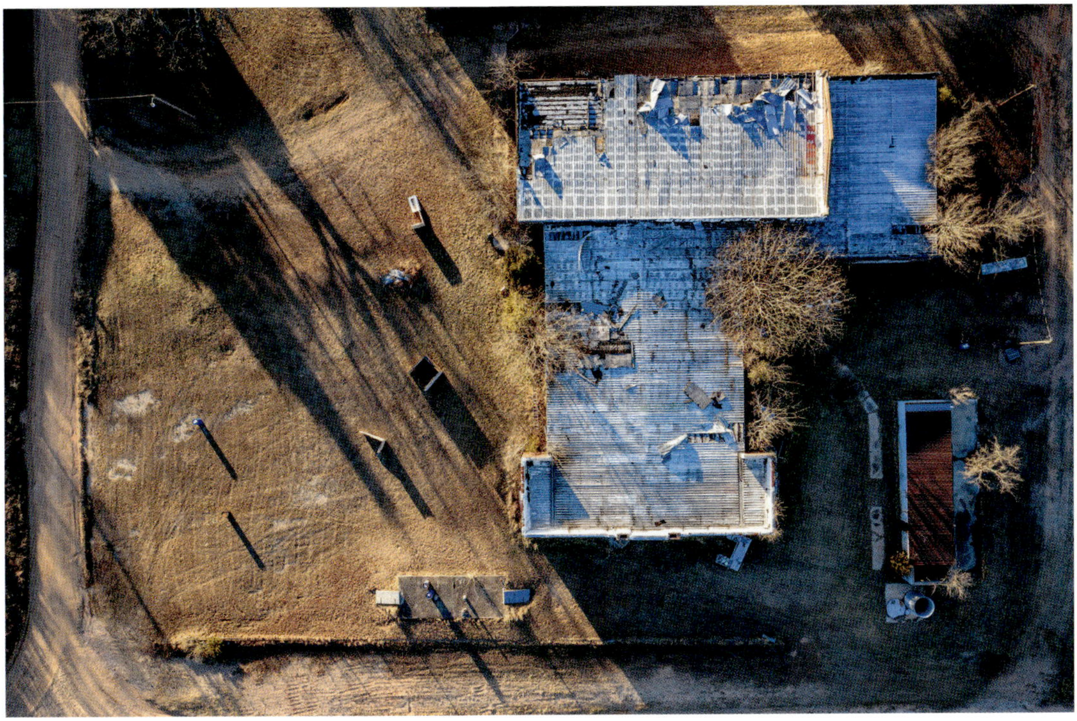

Consolidated Dist. No. 5 from above. The northern gable of the auditorium is still present, indicating the roof was taller at one time.

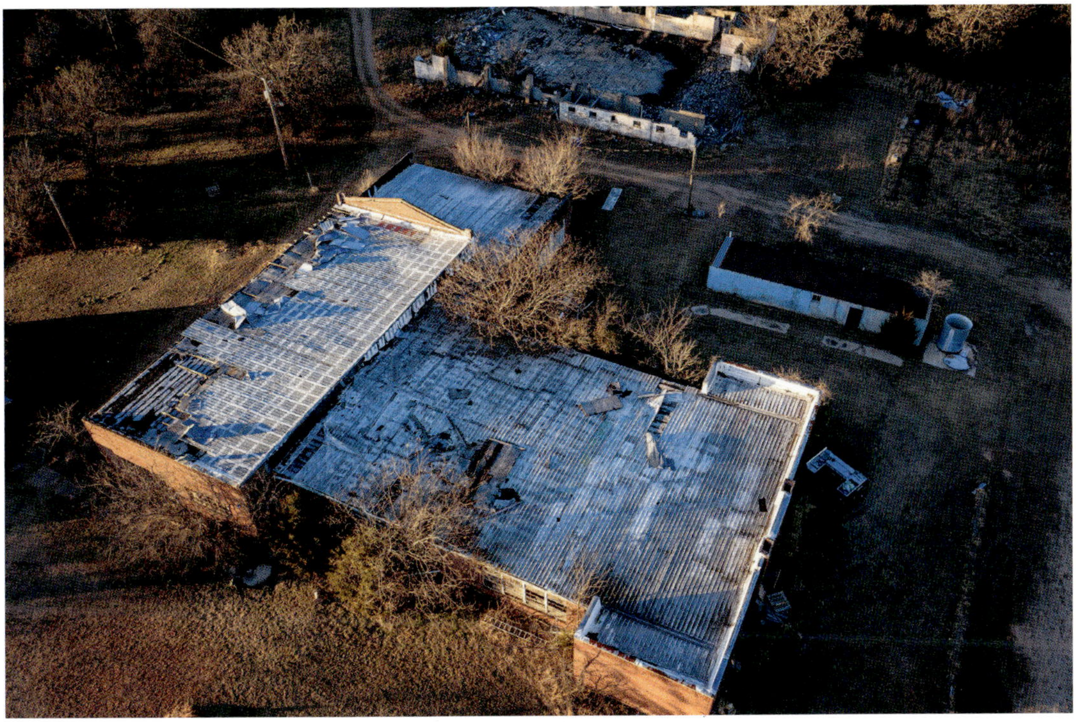

The extent of the damage to the gym, as is the immensity of its size, is also more apparent from above. It is hard to discern from the ground and amongst the rubble how large the facility was. It is close to the footprint size of the main building. These are most likely the first aerial images of the school.

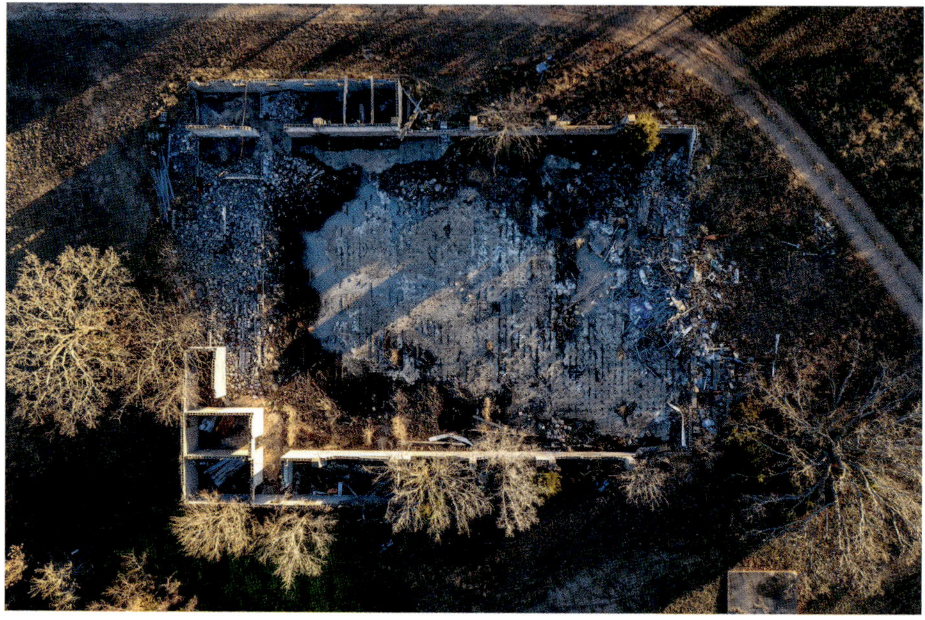

The extent of the damage to the gym, as well as its size, is more evident from aerial images.

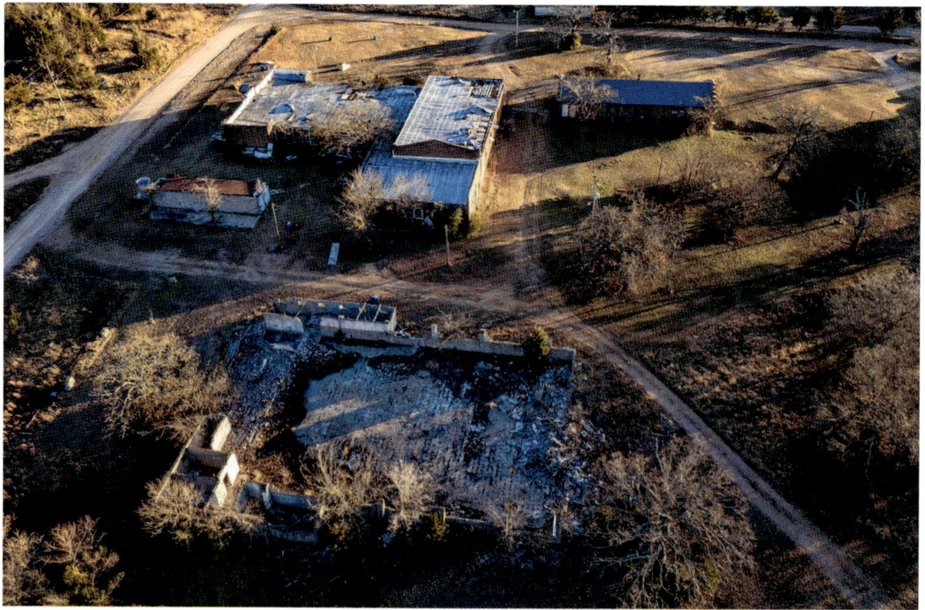

Aerial views also provide a sense of scale regarding how sparsely populated the town of Harjo is. A cluster of homes is on the north end of town, and a few others are scattered throughout. It is hard to imagine that this was once an area that supported over 3,000 people.

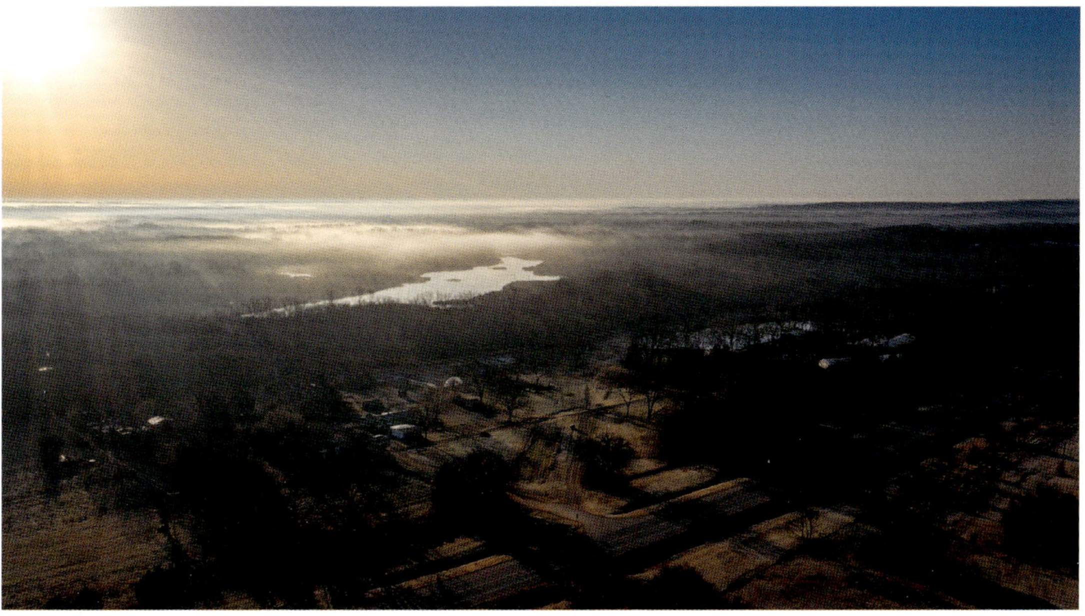

A foggy morning above the town of Harjo. The majority of the town resides in this small cluster of homes.

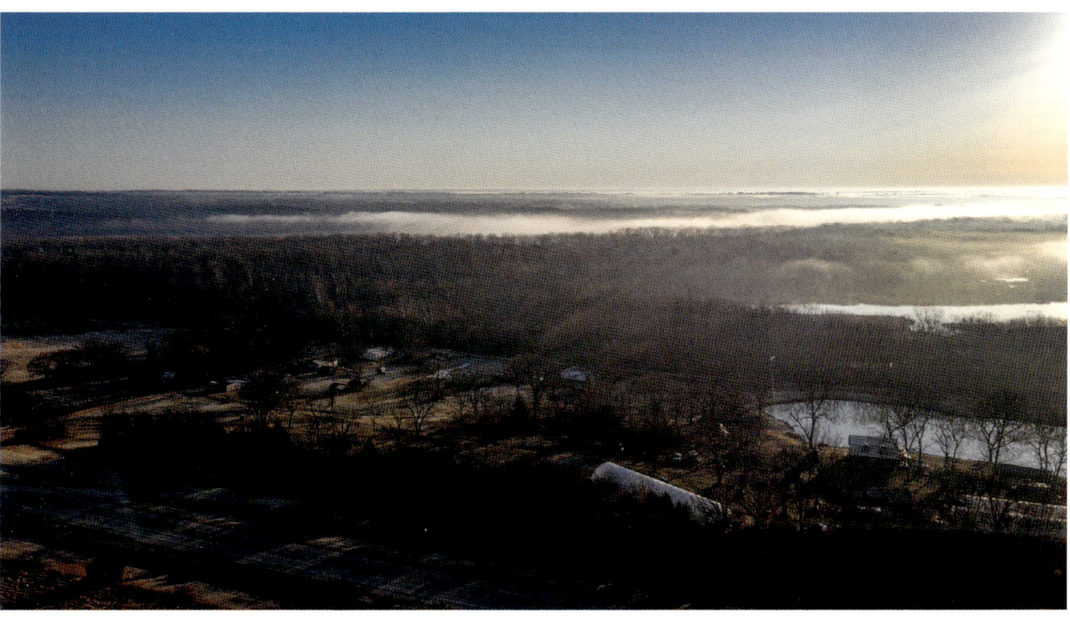

# 6

# THE DECAY OF THE AMERICAN EDUCATION SYSTEM

There has been an ongoing war in American public education. Over the years, we have seen battles unfold which have sought to deconstruct many of these institutions. Oklahoma ranks in the top eight states with an exuberant number of school districts with over 540; however, in 2019, Oklahoma ranked forty-seventh in education. From single-room schoolhouses to consolidated districts, the state's number of closed schools is staggering. The reasons for closure can be wide-ranging.[1, 2]

## Why Consolidate?

States may opt to consolidate districts for any number of reasons. In some cases, it may be to combine more than one district to create a unified administration. Administrative duties can be combined for fiscal benefits. Consolidation is also a means to combine multiple educational resources. For example, a given institution may not have programs such as music or the arts, whereas a larger district may have the capability to offer these beneficial programs. Some districts provide better access to quality education for minority groups. However, consolidation can also mean increased travel for some. While not always the case, some smaller schools could close in the process.[3]

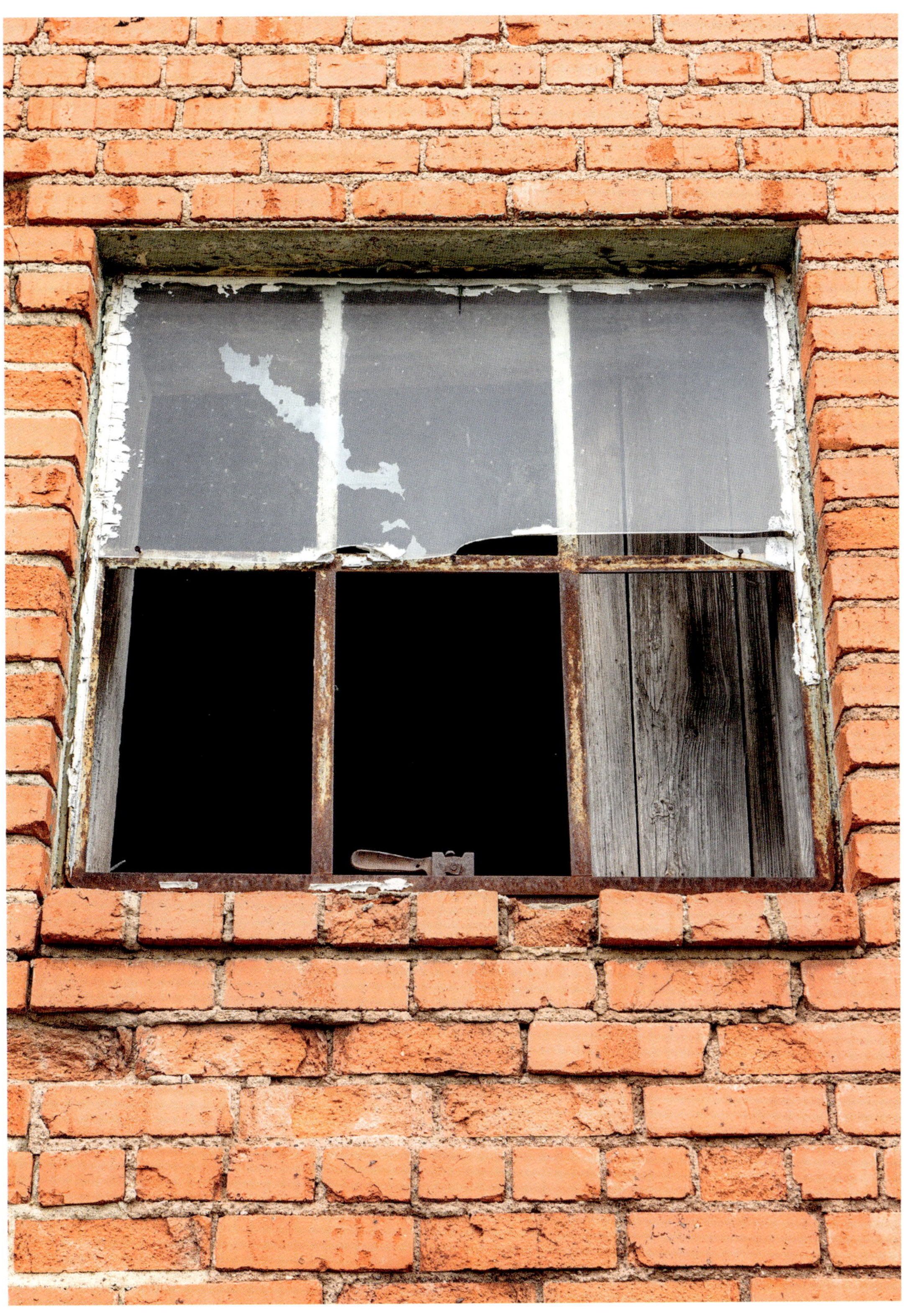

Outside of the auditorium.

## School Closures

School closures across the nation are common, and the situation is not unique to Oklahoma. Since 2002, New York City closed, was in the process of closing, or considered closing ninety-one schools. In 2020, Chicago was in the process of consolidating fourteen schools. The reasons for closure can vary significantly from one district to the next and from state to state.[4]

New York public schools cited poor performance as one of the leading causes for school closure. This can equate to lower than expected graduation rates and declining enrollments. Low standardized testing scores may also play a factor. Generally, these issues, combined with parental dissatisfaction, can lead to a given facility's closure. In rural areas, outdated facilities combined with low enrollment numbers may be to blame. Often more impoverished communities lack funding to make necessary updates in technology. States may also opt to close a given school to clean house and weed out poor teacher performance.[5]

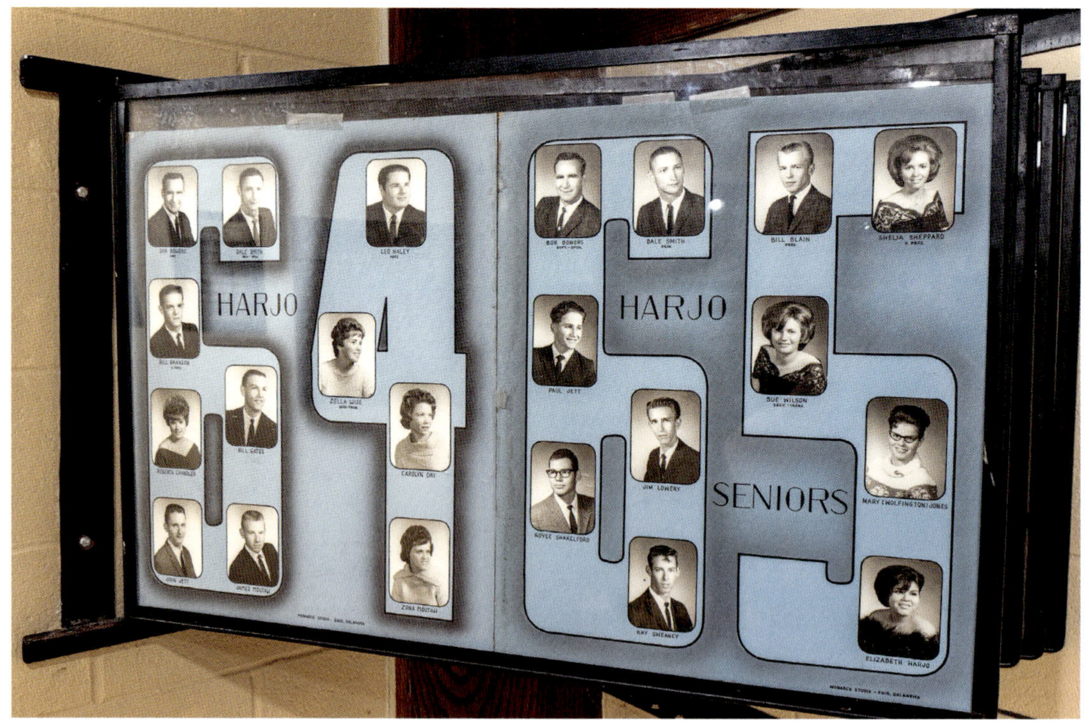


A collection of graduating class photos from various years have a new home at a community center in neighboring Maud.

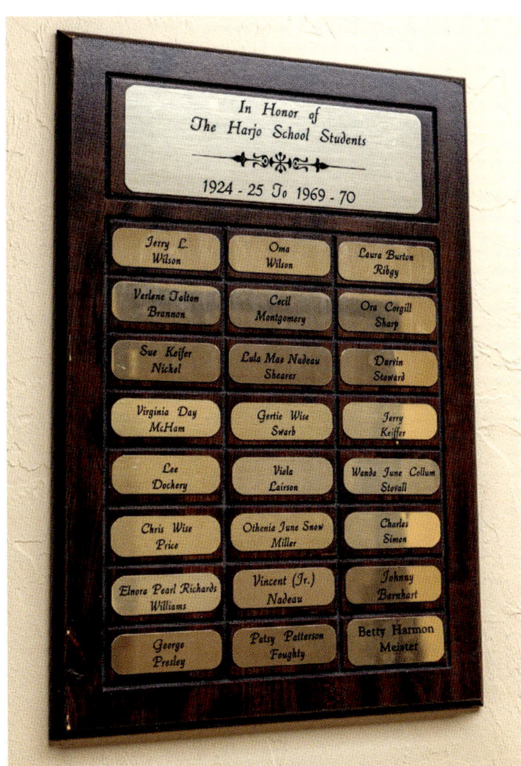


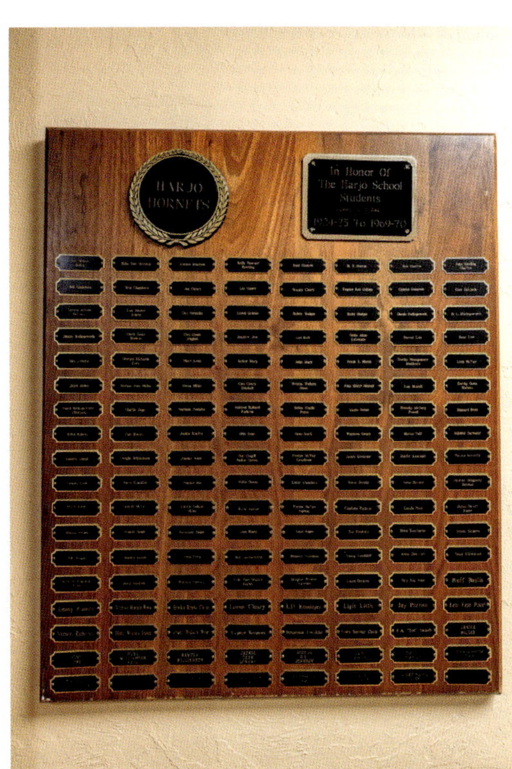


An array of plaques line the walls of a local community center honoring veterans and former students who have passed.

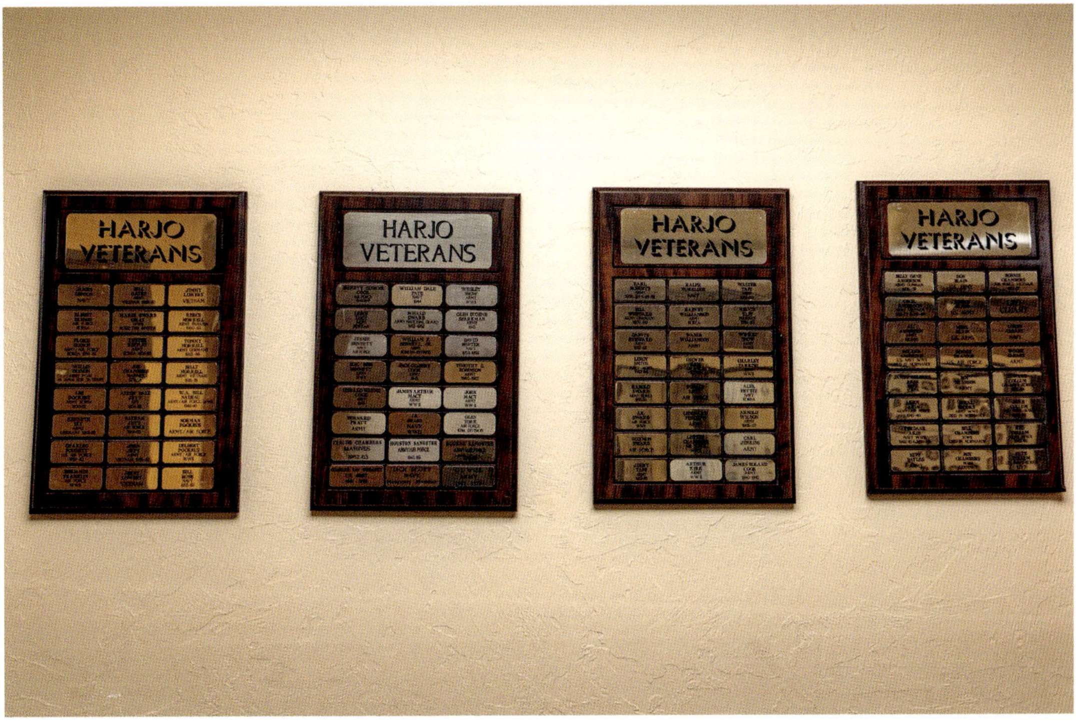

A school's distance from students also plays a role in school closings. In the case of Harjo and other similarly consolidated schools in Oklahoma, students may be bussed in from significant distances. Budgeting issues could make school transportation problematic, leaving parents with the burden to provide transportation. Property values are also directly tied to the educational value within a given district.

Politics are often one of the main factors that affect public education. Skirmishes ensue along party lines debating issues that include increased spending, to deferring control to local municipalities. Equity and quality of education are afterthoughts. School districts do not wield the same influence that lobbyists and special interest groups have when swaying politicians. The inability to lobby effectively directly affects educational spending. Are the voters or the politicians to blame?[6]

## Charter, Public, or Private

One of the more recent issues has been the push for charter schools and privatization. Public schools rely heavily on state and federal funding to survive. However, these funds can be drastically reduced or cut altogether. Federal and state guidelines can also dictate to public institutions what their curriculum should be.[7]

Private schools, however, rely on securing their own funding. Sources may include grants, endowments, donations, and tuition fees. Private schools can offer an array of curriculum that would not normally be permitted in public education systems. For example, private schools may choose to teach religion-based education. Private institutions tend to be more autonomous, have smaller student bodies, and rigorous application and admissions criteria.[8]

Charter schools are a hybrid educational system. Like public schools, charter institutions are free and bared from discriminatory practices. However, there is an application process similar to private schools. Enrollment is also generally limited. Charter schools are usually managed by private for-profit companies.[9]

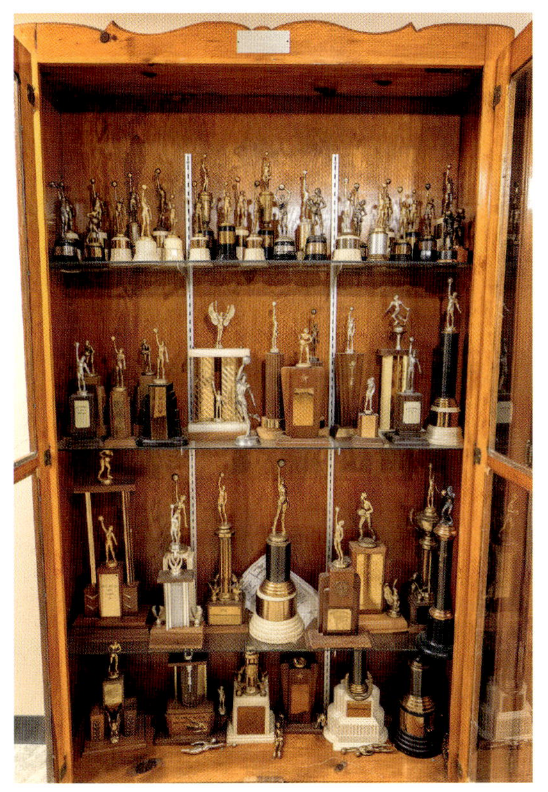

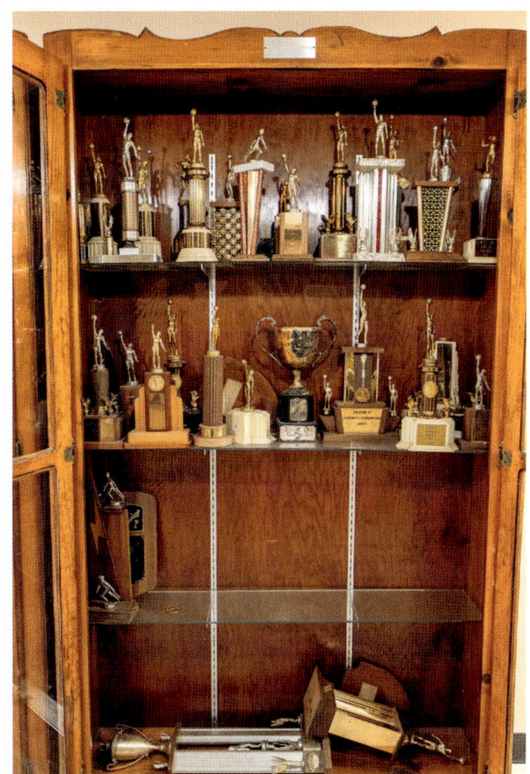

Several school trophies have survived over the years. Those that have been salvaged found a new home at the Maud community center.

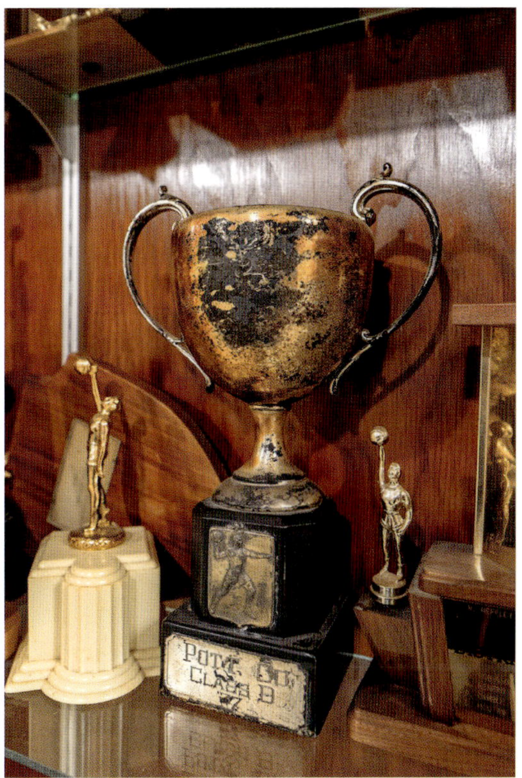

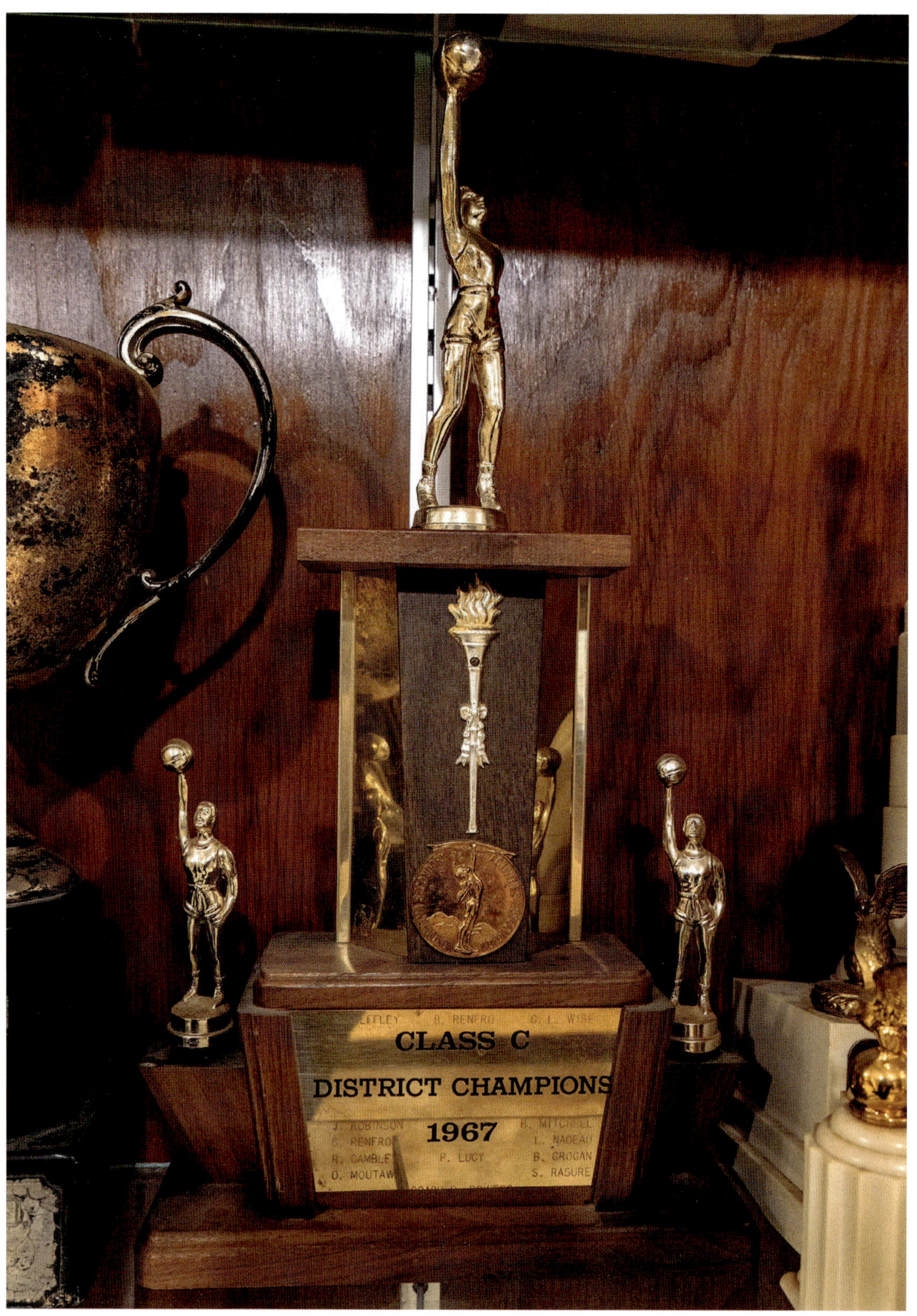


The last trophy was brought home in 1967 for winning the district championship in basketball.

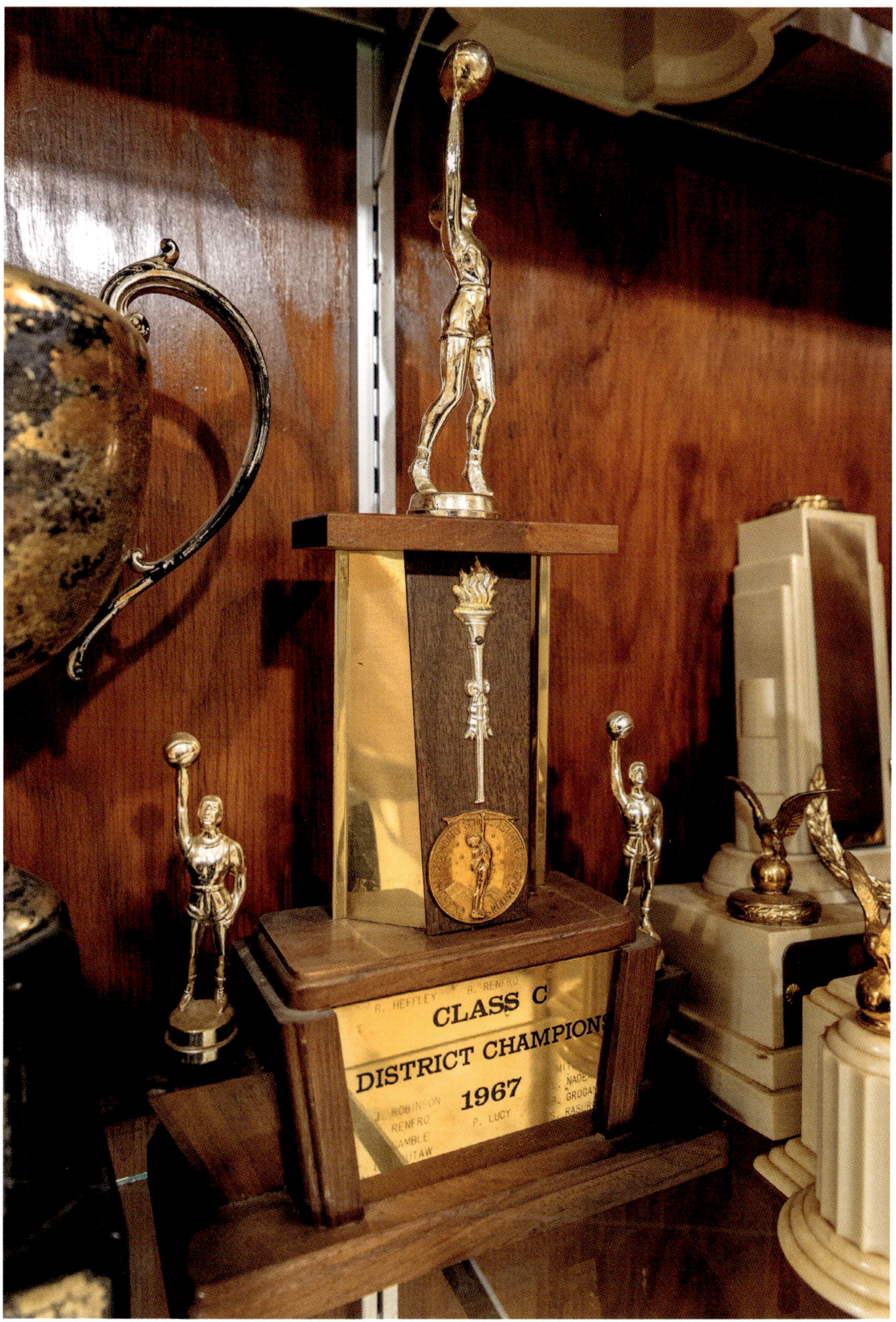
R. HEFFLEY B. RENFRO
CLASS C
DISTRICT CHAMPIONS
1967
J. ROBINSON
P. LUCY

# 7

# THE DISENFRANCHISED

Harjo served some of the most impoverished communities. Much of Oklahoma is rural, and it is not uncommon for there to be 30 miles or more between towns. Schools like Harjo often service students and families who cannot attend schools in wealthier communities. Many of these schools served the African and Native American students, the poor, and the disenfranchised.

What could happen when a school closes? In 2013, Philadelphia and Chicago closed several schools that displaced over 20,000 students, of which approximately 90 percent were from low-income, African American, and Latino households.[1] If this is the effect in large cities, then the statics could be much higher in areas like Oklahoma, where large segments of the population live in rural communities, are from one of the demographics likely to suffer, or from other minority households. This means that in many cases, when schools like Harjo close, those students will be disenfranchised. They are cheated out of education, and families are forced to make the difficult decision of homeschooling, commuting longer distances to the next closest district, or forgo education altogether.

Schools across American are closing at alarming rates. During 2019–2020, forty-three states closed schools for various reasons. These were often closures that affected smaller communities. However, more recent closures affected larger communities, and the changes are becoming permanent.[2] Often, people fail to understand how closing a school impacts a local community and its economy.

Are the parents to blame? This is a looming question. One in five parents believes the responsibility for a child's education rests on the shoulders of local districts, state and federal agencies, and teachers. Historically parents have neglected to hold any of these individuals responsible through the means within their control: voting to correct the issue.[3]

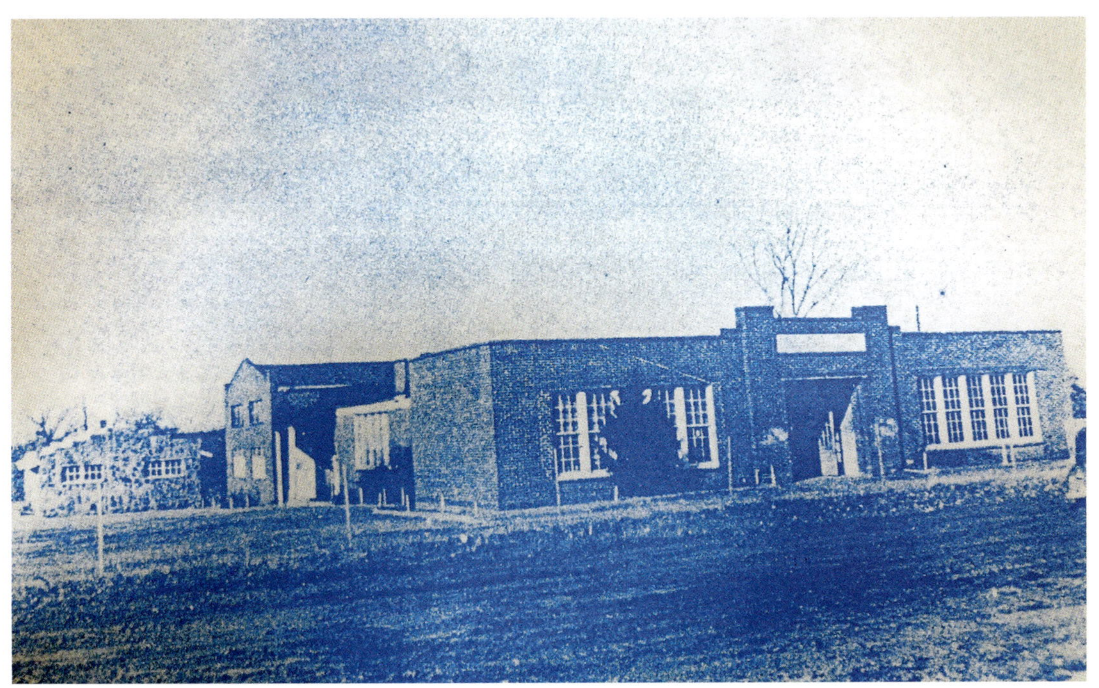

A ditto of the school with the original roof. In this photograph, the auditorium roof was much taller, and the south gable is visible.

Sadly, Harjo is one of many schools in Oklahoma to suffer the same fate as others in the state and throughout the U.S. At one time, Oklahoma was known for its school systems. However, many of these districts were consolidated or simply disappeared for one reason or another. It is a problem that lies within the education system in the U.S. and is not going away. Harjo and its students inevitably became another victim of injustice in the education system.

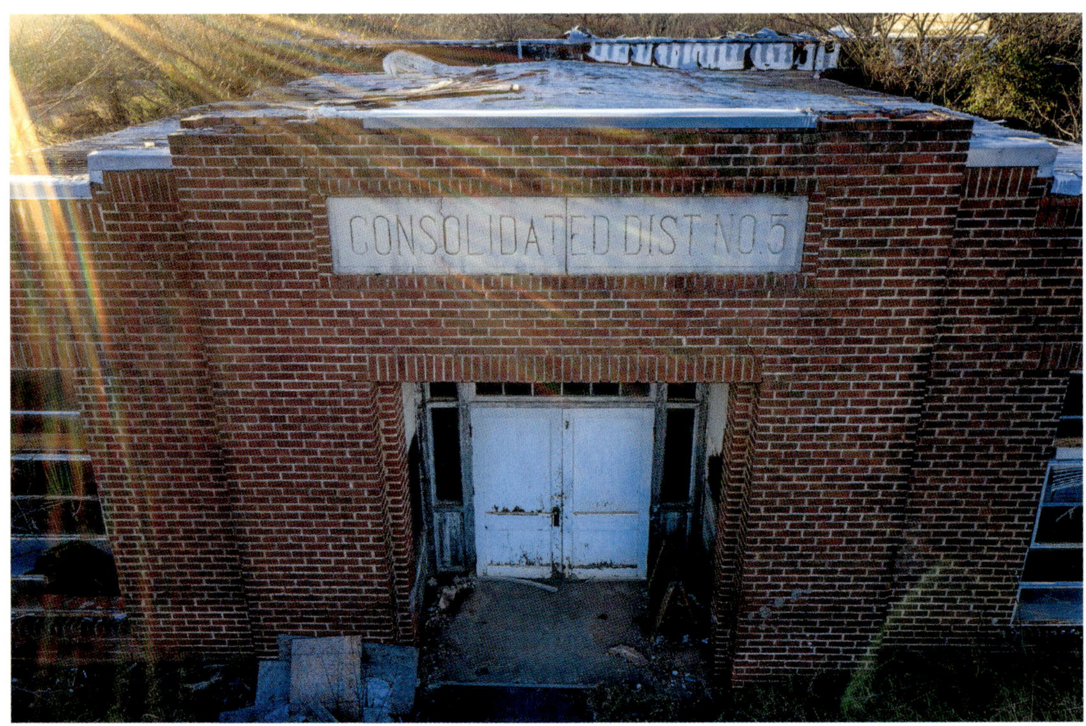


Consolidated Dist. No. 5.

# ENDNOTES

## CHAPTER 1

1 Abandoned Rails, “The Oklahoma City, Ada, and Atoka Railway.”

## CHAPTER 2

1 Tecumseh Oil Record, “Harjo Has Excellent School.”
2 *Ibid.*
3 Karen Bowden, Quentin Blaine, and Stephen Marini, “Town History Guide, New Hampshire Almanac.”
4 Bureau of the Census, “Census Designated Places (CDPs) for the 2020 Census-Final Criteria.”
5 Danielle M. Purifoy, “Living Unincorporated.”
6 RoadsideThoughts, “Census Data for Harjo…”

## CHAPTER 3

1 Spencer J. Macxy, “The Teacherage in American Rural Education.”
2 *Ibid.*
3 *Ibid.*
4 *Ibid.*

## CHAPTER 4

1 Ashley Mattingley, “Question 22: 1940 Census Provides a Glimpse of the Demographics of the New Deal.”
2 *Ibid.*
3 *Ibid.*

## CHAPTER 6

1 National Center for Education Statistics, "Number of Public School Districts, by Local Code (CCD) and State: 2003-2004."
2 Andrea Eager, ""Oklahoma Slips to 47th in Nation on Annual Educational Quality Rankings."
3 Katherine Barrett and Richard Greene, "Why Schools Resist Consolidating."
4 *Ibid.*
5 Grace Chen, ""Why Public Schools Across the Country are Closing Their Campuses."
6 Peter Cunningham, ""Is Politics the Problem or in Education or the Solution?"
7 Psyche Pascual. "Public vs. Private vs. Charter Schools."
8 *Ibid.*
9 *Ibid.*

## CHAPTER 7

1 Brentin Mock "What Happens to Democracy When Schools Close?
2 *Ibid.*
3 Peter Cunningham, "Is Politics the Problem or in Education or the Solution?"

# BIBLIOGRAPHY


Barrett, K., and Greene, R., "Why Schools Resist Consolidating," Governing, October 2014, www.governing.com/archive/gov-school-consolidation-wars.html

Bowden, K., Blaine, Q., and Marini, S., "Town History Guide, New Hampshire Almanac," accessed March 8, 2021, www.nh.gov/almanac/guide.htm

Bureau of the Census, "Census Designated Places (CDPs) for the 2020 Census-Final Criteria," Federal Register, 2018, www.federalregister.gov/documents/2018/11/13/2018-24571/census-designated-places-cdps-for-the-2020-census-final-criteria

"Census Data for Harjo..." RoadsideThoughts, accessed March 8, 2021, roadsidethoughts.com/ok/harjo-xx-pottawatomie-census.htm

Chen, G., "Why Public Schools Across the Country are Closing Their Campuses," Public School Review, May 5, 2020, www.publicschoolreview.com/blog/why-public-schools-across-the-country-are-closing-their-campuses

Cunningham, P., "Is Politics the Problem or in Education or the Solution?" *Education Post*, April 13, 2017, educationpost.org/is-politics-the-problem-in-education-or-the-solution/

Eager, A., "Oklahoma Slips to 47th in Nation on Annual Educational Quality Rankings," *Tulsa World*, January 4, 2017, tulsaworld.com/news/local/education/oklahoma-slips-to-47th-in-nation-on-annual-educational-quality-ranking/article_0053bd86-0819-5cab-8eda-2edcfbff0594.html

"Harjo Has Excellent School," *Tecumseh Oil Record*, February 14, 1929, 1(4), p. 5, gateway.okhistory.org/ark:/67531/metadc407083/m1/5/zoom/?resolution=3&lat=3060&lon=2144

Mattingly, A., "Question 22: 1940 Census Provides a Glimpse of the Demographics of the New Deal," *Prologue Magazine,* 2012, 44(2), www.archives.gov/publications/prologue/2012/summer/question22.html

Maxcy, S. J., "The Teacherage in American Rural Education," *The Journal of General Education,* (1979) 30(4), 267-274, www.jstor.org/stable/27796717

Mock, B., "What Happens to Democracy When Schools Close?" Bloomberg, May 1, 2020, www.bloomberg.com/news/articles/2020-05-01/how-closing-schools-hurts-democracy

"Number of Public School Districts, by Local Code (CCD) and State: 2003–2004," Rural Education in America, *National Center for Education Statistics*, accessed March 8, 2021, nces.ed.gov/surveys/ruraled/TablesHTML/5localedistricts.asp

Purifoy, D. M., "Living Unincorporated," Duke Human Rights Center, accessed March 8, 2021, humanrights.fhi.duke.edu/living-unincorporated/

Pascual, P., "Public vs. Private vs. Charter Schools," Great Schools.org, December 3, 2012, www.greatschools.org/gk/articles/public-private-charter-schools/

"The Oklahoma City, Ada, and Atoka Railway," Abandoned Rails, accessed March 8, 2021, www.abandonedrails.com/oklahoma-city-to-atoka-and-ada